A History of Canadian Gardening

BY
CAROL MARTIN

McArthur & Company

Toronto

First published in Canada by McArthur & Company, 2000

Canadian Cataloguing in Publication Data

Martin, Carol
History of Canadian gardening

ISBN 1-55278-167-4

1. Gardening – Canada – History. 2. Gardening – Canada – History – Pictorial works. 3. Gardens – Canada – History. 4.Gardens – Canada – History – Pictorial works. I. Title.

SB451.36.C3M37 2000   635'.0971   C00-931336-2

Design: Miriam Bloom, Expression Communications Inc.
Printed in Canada by St. Joseph M.O.M. Printing (Ontario)

Cover Illustration: *La Propriété de l'artiste, à Gentilly*, c. 1853, Joseph Légaré. La Collection Lavalin du Musée d'art contemporain de Montréal. Photo: Richard-Max Tremblay
p. i: Archives of Ontario C 130-1-0-3-5
p. ii: VanDusen Botanical Garden/Photograph by David Jones
p. vii: Frère Marie-Victorin, *Flore laurentienne* (Montreal: LaSalle, 1935), detail 335/National Library of Canada 22205
p. viii: Agriculture and Agri-Food Canada
Endpapers: Centre for Canadian Historical Horticultural Studies, Royal Botanical Gardens, Hamilton, Ontario

McArthur & Company
322 King Street West, Suite 402
Toronto, ON, M5V 1J2

10 9 8 7 6 5 4 3 2 1

The publisher would like to acknowledge the financial support of the Government of Canada through the Book Publishing Industry Development Program (BPIDIP) for our publishing activities. The publisher further wishes to acknowledge the financial support of the Ontario Arts Council for our publishing program.

To my parents:
Thomas Charles and Janet Doris Wood (née Hudson),
who first introduced me to
the fascinating world of gardening;
and to my children:
Pamela, Christopher and Jeremy,
with thanks for their contributions

Contents

Preface

LIKE MANY CANADIANS I have gardened, in one form or another, all my life. In 1950, when I was a teenager, my parents bought five acres just outside Ottawa, and here they were able to indulge their own love of gardening. They had a large vegetable garden with rows of raspberries, beds of strawberries and asparagus, and all kinds of annual vegetables. My mother loved to experiment, so we were introduced to many things, such as Chinese cabbage, that were not available in our local stores at that time. And, of course, the house was surrounded by flower beds.

When I was raising my own family, our house was on a small lot in downtown Toronto, and there seemed little scope for gardening. Nevertheless, we struggled to raise our tomatoes, lettuce and radishes in the rubble and ashes that passed for soil in the backyard. The front walk was edged with homemade flower boxes. One summer my sons and I became gardeners at an allotment plot outside the city, driving thirty miles to a rocky, barren field with no access to water. Here,

with other hopeful city dwellers, we attempted to supply the family with fresh vegetables. Not surprisingly, the experiment was something of a failure.

In spite of these experiences, wherever I was over the following decades I always had something growing—windows full of house plants in apartments, raised vegetable beds and perennial borders on an acre in Quebec outside Ottawa, trees, shrubs and native flowers where I now live in southern Ontario.

In the 1990s I was freelancing, and part of my work involved organizing exhibitions for the National Library of Canada. It was wonderfully interesting work that took advantage of my lifelong interest in books and publishing. This was at a time when Canadians were beginning to publish a broad array of gardening books, and when I suggested an exhibition on the subject, the library agreed.

I knew that there were enough new books to make an interesting display and that there were enough people interested in gardening to attract an audience. What I didn't then know was what a fascinating historical subject an exhibition of garden materials could make.

My personal knowledge of Canadian books on gardening went back about thirty years. I certainly knew of *Chatelaine's Gardening Book* by Lois Wilson, published in 1970, but what I remembered about my parents' search for information was that anything they found turned out to be geared to the climate in the United States or England. The only Canadian information available was in the pamphlets put out by the Central Experimental Farm.

When I began researching for the exhibition, two resources were particularly helpful. One was the pioneering work on the subject done by Edwinna von Baeyer. Not only had she written *Rhetoric and Roses: A History of Canadian Gardening 1900-1930*, but her bibliographic research in *A Selected Bibliography for Garden History in Canada* was invaluable. The second essential resource came in the person of Toronto landscape historian Pleasance Crawford. Early on she invited me into her extensive garden library and devoted a morning to leading me through the subject. I'm grateful to both of these women. Their mutual interest led them to edit a book together a few years later, *Garden Voices: Two Centuries of Canadian Garden Writing*.

The more research I undertook for the exhibition, the more fascinated I became with how a study of Canada's garden history opened up a unique view of the country's social history. I decided to continue to study the subject and eventually to write this book. Beyond the few books listed above, material on the subject was scattered and often difficult to come by. To my surprise, few general histories of Canada mention gardening at all—an activity that has been important, even essential, to our survival. But in specialized books and in early letters and journals there were often enticing stories, although even pioneer material often gave only a glancing mention to work in the garden. Probably because it was such a normal part of life.

On the positive side, people have been writing about how to grow flowers, vegetables, trees and shrubs for more than a hundred years, and I have learned a great deal from these early works. In many ways, gardening has changed very little over the decades and centuries. Even many of the tools remain basically the same. Hundreds of years ago, Native people practised companion planting, as many of us do today. We still plant cabbages, potatoes and peas (although recent immigrants have broadened our choices). The morning glories mentioned by Ontario pioneer Catharine Parr Traill can still be found in gardens, and many gardeners are now going back to earlier varieties of favourite flowers. Hoes, trowels and rakes used by modern gardeners remain essentially the same.

I visited many of the libraries, archives and public gardens in the country, in person when that was possible, or by telephone, letter, fax, e-mail or through the Internet. Many of their names appear on the credits below the illustrations I have included in the book. Of them all, I am most indebted to Linda Brownlee at the library of the Royal Botanical Gardens in Hamilton. The RBG houses an excellent library and archive that is indispensable to a garden researcher. I visited the RBG a number of times, and Linda was always ready to help me search for specific subjects, books or periodicals. The seed catalogue collection is particularly valuable, as is the complete collection of *Canadian Horticulturist*.

Of course, the mainstay of my research was the collection at the National Library of Canada itself. There I worked closely with Andrea Paradis, then Exhibitions and Liaison Officer, who was always helpful in advising me about the intricacies of exhibitions, and in the process, she became a friend. The library's task is to collect all Canadian publications. Most of the books and magazines I needed to review, and eventually include in the exhibition, were available there. The exhibition, "Cultivating Canadian Gardens: The History of Gardening in Canada," ran for most of 1998 and is still available on the library's web site.

The whole staff at the National Library of Canada has been of great help in the researching of this book. In addition to Andrea Paradis, I am particularly grateful to Mary Jane Starr, Randall Ware, Michel Brisebois, Margo Wiper and Dale Simmons.

I would like to thank the following for special assistance and ideas along the way: Heather Apple of Seeds of Diversity, Dennis Pollock at Black Creek Pioneer Village, Janina Stensson of the Dunington-Grubb & Stensson Collection at the University of Guelph Library, Philip Cercone and Arden Ford of McGill-Queen's University Press, Marjorie Ford of Halifax, and Bruce Whiteman then at McGill University.

I am especially grateful to the friends and family who took care of me as I travelled across the country and were willing to discuss my research along the way: Sheila Fischman and Donald Winkler in Montreal; Janet Lunn, Jocelyn Harvey and Miriam and Victor Rabinovitch in Ottawa; Mike and Fran Preston in Toronto; Bill Smyth in Hamilton; Frank Wood and Betty Verkuil in Vancouver; and Valerie Wyatt and Larry MacDonald in Victoria.

Finally, my thanks to Edwinna von Baeyer and Nancy Newman for their comments on the manuscript; to my editor, Linda Biesenthal, for her helpful advice and skilful editing; and to the designer of this book, Miriam Bloom, for her sensitive treatment of the material.

1
Canada's First Gardeners

LIVING IN HARMONY WITH THE LAND

The original inhabitants of North America felt a close relationship to the natural world around them. Plants, animals and people all had souls in this world, and there was a strong spiritual connection between the people, the food they ate and the plants, fish and animals that supplied everything they needed. Originally, they were nomadic and moved according to the availability of food. On the coasts, the sea provided much of what was needed for a good life; on the prairies, almost everything came from the buffalo; in the east, there was an abundance of deer, fish and plants.

The Ojibwa gathered wild rice in the fall, beating the kernels into their canoes while gliding through the shallow waters.

Drawing by Seth Eastman in *Ethnological Research, Respecting the Red Man of America* (Bureau of Indian Affairs, 1853), plate 4/Toronto Reference Library

All Native peoples were to some degree hunters and gatherers, and plants from the wild were an important part of their diet. Olive Patricia Dickason, who has written frequently about the Amerindians and their sophisticated knowledge of plants, emphasizes their skill in exploiting the resources of the world around them. It has been estimated, for instance, that more than 500 native plant species were used as food and in food preparation, and 500 were used as medicines, as materials or in rituals.

Joseph-François Lafitau was a Jesuit who spent five years, from 1713 to 1718, in New France near present-day Caughnawauga studying the Iroquois. In his book *Customs of the American Indians Compared with Customs of Primitive Times*, he noted the wonderful success the Iroquois had in healing wounds with the medicines they made based on such plants as blue lobelia (*Lobelia siphilitica*), sassafras (*Sassafras officinale*) and cardinal flower (*Lobelia cardinalis*). Wood and bark, especially from the birch (*Betula papyrifera*),

The Saskatoon berry (*Amelanchier alnifolia*) was important to the diet of Native people living on the prairies. The berries were pounded together with fat and dried buffalo meat to make pemmican, a compact, high-protein, easily transported food. As seen here, the berries were dried by laying them out in the sun.

National Archives of Canada/PA-044566

were used as fuel and for making canoes, tools and boxes. Fibres from roots and from the husks and stems of corn were woven into baskets and twisted into rope or twine. Dyes were made from numerous plants, such as jewelweed or touch-me-not (*Impatiens capensis*) and the bark of the butternut tree (*Juglans cinerea*). Tobacco was one of the most important plants used in rituals or as a gift of thanks to the spirit world, particularly among the Huron.

Although the Native diet was supplemented with plants gathered from the wild, such as nuts, berries, wild crabapples, mushrooms, ferns, rhizomes, roots and seaweed, harvesting these foods was not necessarily a matter of luck. Sometimes these wild foods came from nurtured groves or patches that were considered the preserve of an individual family or community, and were cultivated by them.

Wherever they grew, wild berries added a welcome change as well as vitamins and minerals to early diets. They were eaten fresh and dried and were preserved using methods that had been developed over the years. On the prairies, for example, silver buffaloberries (*Shepherdia argentea*) were used to flavour buffalo meat. In British Columbia, the related soapberry (*Shepherdia canadensis*) was beaten with water and sweetened to make a frothy delicacy, still sometimes eaten today. The Saskatoon berry (*Amelanchier alnifolia*), which gave the city of Saskatoon its name and which grows across the prairies from western Ontario to the Yukon, was mixed with dried meat and fat to make pemmican, a valuable preserved food that Native people introduced to the early voyageurs. For these travellers, it was the ideal food to take on their long, arduous trips. And, as today, gooseberries, currants, cranberries, strawberries and many varieties of raspberries were enjoyed in season.

Along the west coast, the bulb of the blue camas (*Camassia quamash*), a member of the lily family, was a staple wherever it could be found. On Vancouver Island, the Coast Salish cultivated and harvested the plants:

> They divided the camas beds into individually owned plots, passed from generation to generation. Each season, the families cleared their plots of stones, weeds and brush, often by controlled burning. Harvesting took several days, with entire families participating. The harvesters systematically lifted the soil in small sections, removed the larger bulbs and replaced the sod. Even in this century, families would collect four to five potato-sacks full at a time.[1]

In a similar way, other coastal groups tended and harvested rhizomes of springbank clover (*Trifolium wormskjoldii*), another important vegetable.

Farther west on the plains, the hunters gathered, dried and pulverized prairie turnips (*Psoralea escu-lenta*), a good source of vitamin C during the winter months. According to Dickason, "there is also some evidence that they moved plant stocks from one location to another."[2] Henry Youle Hind, a naturalist who accompanied expeditions to the prairies in 1857 and 1858 as a scientific observer, described how the many bushels of turnips collected by the Cree women and children were used:

> The Crees consume this important vegetable in various ways; they eat it uncooked, or they boil it, or roast it in the embers, or dry it, and crush it to a powder and make soup of it. Large quantities are stored in buffalo skin bags for winter use.[3]

From Manitoba east, the grains of wild rice (*Zizania aquatica*), a tall grass that grows in shallow waters, were harvested and eaten by the Ojibwa. They nurtured the crop, weeding the beds and bundling the stocks before the seeds were ripe to discourage pests and retain the grain until it could be harvested. "Bundling also permitted easier access to the rice by creating pathways through the denser stands and was used by the Ojibwa to establish property rights to this resource."[4] Care was taken while harvesting to scatter enough seed in the beds to ensure a good crop the following year. After European immigration, as the Ojibwa were forced farther west, they extended the range of wild rice by establishing new stands in

The Coast Salish of Vancouver Island maintained and harvested the blue camas (*Camassia quamash*), a practice that can be called semi-agricultural. They steamed the bulbs in large pits and used them to sweeten dishes before sugar arrived on the west coast.

Photographs by R.D. and N.J. Turner

Salmonberry (*Rubus spectabilis* Pursh) is a raspberry-like plant that grows along the west coast. The coastal Native people ate the berries and the green sprouts of the plant, usually with salmon. These early ripening, juicy berries range in colour from bright gold to deep red.

Photograph by R.D. and N.J. Turner

appropriate environments. This same wild rice is harvested and sold as a specialty grain today.

Long before the Europeans arrived, many of the Iroquoian people of the St. Lawrence and Great Lakes region had become serious farmers and were growing food, not only for the use of the community but also to trade for other goods. Their most important crop was maize, or corn (*Zea mays*), which had first been domesticated in Central America about 5000 BC. From there the crop had gradually spread northward until it reached its climatic limit in what is now southern Ontario and the southeast corner of Manitoba. By the sixteenth century, there were about 150 different varieties of corn. The kind grown in what is now Canada, perhaps as early as AD 600, was probably Northern Flint. Gradually over the next 700 years, beans (*Phaseolus vulgaris*), tobacco (*Nicotiana tabacum*), sunflowers (*Helianthus annuus*) and squash (*Cucurbita pepo*) were added to the gardens.

Corn and beans remained by far the most important crops cultivated by Native communities here, and as agriculture became more and more central to their way of life, the communities became more settled and their numbers grew. By the fifteenth century, the Huron were living in villages of a thousand people or more. These agricultural settlements stretched as far east as Hochelaga (Montreal) and even Stadacona (Quebec City).

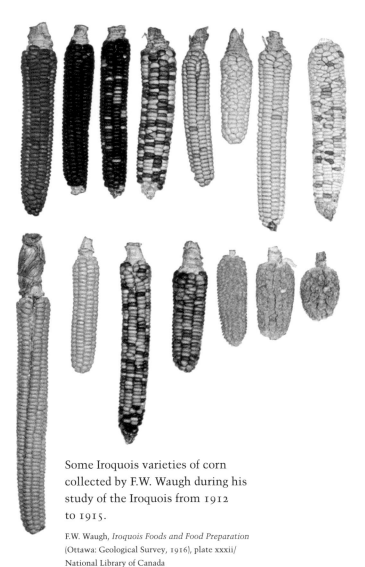

Some Iroquois varieties of corn collected by F.W. Waugh during his study of the Iroquois from 1912 to 1915.

F.W. Waugh, *Iroquois Foods and Food Preparation* (Ottawa: Geological Survey, 1916), plate xxxii/ National Library of Canada

HURONIA

Huronia, the homeland of the Huron in the sixteenth and seventeenth centuries, lay between Lake Simcoe and Georgian Bay. It is estimated that twenty to thirty thousand people lived here in some twenty villages. They were highly successful gardeners who concentrated mainly on the Three Sisters—corn, beans and squash. According to some estimates, the Huron grew fifteen varieties of corn, sixty varieties of beans and eight varieties of squash.[5] The seeds of all three were planted together in hills. As the corn grew tall and strong, the beans twined around the stalks (fixing nitrogen and thus improving the soil), and the squash spread its broad leaves on the ground at the base of the corn, thereby controlling the weeds. This is an excellent example of what we call companion planting today. When the three vegetables were cooked together in a Native dish known in some places as succotash, the corn and beans provided a complete protein.

The good soil and rolling hills of southwestern Ontario provided excellent fields for the Hurons. They cleared the bush using a slash-and-burn technique. The men girdled the trees and lit a fire around the base of each trunk while the women gathered the smaller branches for firewood.

Corn is believed to have originated in the highlands of Central America. Over thousands of years, Amerindians nurtured the original tiny, finger-sized cobs into something closer to what we know today. Gradually the plant made its way north, through Mexico, the southern United States and into southern Ontario. Always it was known as one of the Three Sisters, corn, beans and squash, which were grown and cooked together. Corn, the major crop, was considered sacred, and many stories have been told about its origin. The one most closely associated with the Iroquoian peoples of the north involves the shamanic vision of a gifted young man on a spirit quest to save his starving people. A spirit guide appeared, dressed in yellow and green with a headdress of green feathers, and forced the young man into a wrestling match. When the spirit guide was defeated, a tall green plant sprang up where his body lay. The crop it produced saved the young man and his people from starvation.

Although few of the stories and legends made their way as far as the Hurons, the gardeners honoured the three sisters with dances and festivals to ensure the success of the harvest.

The women were the principal gardeners. They cultivated the land between the stumps with simple hoes made of wood or bone. With the help of the children, they planted the corn (after soaking the seeds for a few days), tended the growing plants and harvested the produce. The soil here was not rich, and although the burning that preceded planting and the Huron's method of only minimally disturbing the ground helped to sustain it, its fertility lasted only four to six years. As the soil became depleted, the crops would be moved to freshly cleared land. It has been estimated that by the early seventeenth century, the Hurons had close to 3000 hectares under cultivation[6]—an astonishing accomplishment for the time.

After the harvest, the corn was dried or ground into meal. It could then be stored, usually in large, protective cavities in the ground. Enough corn was stored to provide seeds for planting and for years when the crops failed. The dried corn was light and easy to carry over long distances, making it valuable both for trading and as food for travelling.

The only crop cultivated by the men was tobacco, which the Hurons used as a sacred plant for ceremonial purposes. Both tobacco and corn were traded for meat and fish with the Algonkins to the north and for furs with other tribes to the west. Jerusalem artichoke (*Helianthus tuberosus*), a native sunflower, was another

The women and children were the cultivators. They planted the crops, protected and nurtured them and did most of the harvesting. Here they can be seen shooing crows away from a cornfield.

Ethnological Research, Respecting the Red Man of America (Bureau of Indian Affairs, 1853), plate 5/Toronto Reference Library

important crop both for the food in its tubers and for the oil that was extracted from the seeds and used in cooking and as a skin cream.

By the time Europeans arrived in North America, there was a very large Native population throughout the territory. "For North America north of the Rio Grande in the early sixteenth century, estimates range up to an unlikely 18 million and even higher."[7] The majority of the Native population in what is now

Canada lived in the successful agricultural communities of southern Ontario and along the west coast where resources were abundant. Diseases previously unknown in North America arrived with the Europeans. Smallpox in particular had a drastic effect on the Native population. It is estimated that more than 90 per cent of the Native people of North America died as a result. Within thirty years, the Huron nation was decimated by disease, war with the Iroquois and, ultimately, starvation: "In little more than a generation Huronia was scattered far and wide, its villages destroyed, its cornfields reverting back to forest."[8] Anthropologist Bruce Trigger has noted: "In 1650 weeds grew in the cornfields of the Huron ... Abandoned hearths, charred poles, and rotting slabs of cedar bark were all that remained of a series of villages that had once been inhabited by over 20,000 people."[9]

Another result of European contact with the Americas was the introduction of a number of important new foods to diets back in Europe. Among these were potatoes, tomatoes, peanuts, pineapples, cacao and corn. In Canada, when the early immigrants faced starvation, Native people introduced them to the tubers of the Jerusalem artichoke, one of the foods that helped them survive. Earlier still, in 1535, Jacques Cartier and his men were treated for scurvy with white cedar (*Thuja occidentalis*).

Huron women grinding and preparing corn.

Father François du Creux, *Historiae Canadensis* ... (Paris, 1664), opposite 22/ National Library of Canada

The sugar maple (*Acer saccharum*) is native to North America, and its sap was treasured by the aboriginal inhabitants for its sweetness. It was used as juice directly from the tree or boiled down to syrup or sugar by adding red-hot stones to the sap, which was stored in birch-bark containers. Maple sugar was a staple of the Native diet and was used as flavouring.

William Morell Harmer Collection/National Archives of Canada/C-019890

Europeans brought the potato to the west coast. The potato became a staple of the Haida and was traded both to other Native communities along the coast and to European sailors.

EARLY LIFE IN THE WEST

Across the prairies, although the buffalo provided early people with almost everything they needed to survive, we know that corn was grown in the most southern region of present-day Manitoba in the sandy soil along the Red River. Archaeological finds in the 1980s at Lockport north of Winnipeg included charred corn, deep bell-shaped storage pits and hoes made of bison scapula (shoulder bone) dating from the early fifteenth century. Similar sites from a later date have been excavated in southwestern Manitoba near the Souris River.

The first written mention of Native agriculture on the prairies after European contact was in 1805 in accounts of the crops of maize and potatoes cultivated by the Netley Creek Odawas. Over the next few decades, beans and squash (or melon) were added to the gardens, which expanded as the Native hunters saw that the days of the great buffalo herds were coming to an end. The gardens were spaced along trade and hunting routes so that provisions would be available where needed. The Odawas shared seed with the Selkirk settlers and provided food to European traders.[10]

Shortly after Confederation in 1867, the Canadian government assumed responsibility for the prairies (previously part of the Northwest Territories) and began a campaign to encourage settlement there. This meant negotiating land agreements with the Plains nations. Throughout the 1870s, treaties were signed with the 35,000 Native people across the region. In addition to the regular terms that had been agreed to in the east, the Native delegations, aware that their traditional hunting lifestyle was on the way out, requested that the Crown provide seeds (wheat, barley, oats and potatoes), hoes, spades, harrows and ploughs for the communities to share, as well as livestock and other farm implements. They also asked for training in farming techniques to help them begin their new settled way of life.

These terms were agreed to, albeit reluctantly, by the Canadian government, but they were fulfilled only sporadically and often in a cursory way. In addition, the Native people were allowed only 160 acres (about 64 hectares) per family of five; unlike the settlers, they were not allowed to acquire additional land. "By 1878 the Plains nations faced disaster because of the government's failure to make significant headway in providing agricultural instruction and the rapidly declining buffalo population."[11] The government later

Native lodges in front of Rocky Mountain Fort. Fur traders across the prairies were dependent on pemmican and other provisions supplied by the Plains buffalo hunters. The Nor'Westers built a series of forts in order to trade for the protein-rich food available from the Plains nations, for whom trading became an alternate way of life.

Painting by Paul Kane, April 1848/National Archives of Canada C-114374

By the late 1880s the Indian Commissioner for the North-West Territories was encouraging Native farmers to work without modern machinery. But hand sowing, as the Blackfoot farmers are doing here, was too labour intensive to be successful on the prairies. It was the government's plan to turn Native people into yeoman farmers who would not compete with the territory's new immigrants. The government also set out to promote individualism among the Native people by discouraging their co-operative way of life.

Glenbow Archives, Calgary, Canada/ NA 127-1

attempted to improve matters by establishing model farms, but the truth was that no one knew much about how to farm on the prairies. "It is one of the tragic ironies of Western Canadian history that former buffalo hunters found themselves in the vanguard of experimental farmers trying to adapt an ancient humid-land agricultural system developed in the Old World to the semi-arid environment of the Canadian prairies."[12] It was only with the development of Marquis wheat (discussed in chapter 7) in 1909 that grain farming on the prairies became successful. Unfortunately, by then the new immigrant settlers resented any moves that allowed the Native growers to compete with their own agricultural efforts.

In *I Have Lived Here Since the World Began*, Arthur J. Ray describes the shameful way the Canadian government lived up to the treaties. The government not only managed to discourage the First Nations from farming communally on their lands and thus take advantage of the expensive equipment required for successful agriculture on the prairies, but actually expropriated reserves or relocated Native groups for the benefit of others. The Métis, in particular, ended up in poverty. Their ancestral hunting life was no longer viable, and they became the target of the racial intolerance of the new settlers:

> In the end, the failure of government agricultural training programs, the loss of reserve lands, and the dispossession of most Métis made many descendants of the Plains nations and the Métis—two of the most powerful nineteenth-century Native groups—into paupers who scratched out a miserable existence on the edges of a land their ancestors had dominated and roamed over freely.[13] 🍃

Some Native farmers worked together and purchased machinery, such as the steam tractor and thresher shown here with Cree farmers at Whitefish Lake in Saskatchewan. The restrictions on credit and selling of produce imposed by the Indian Act, however, made it unlikely that they would become successful farmers.

Glenbow Archives, Calgary, Canada/NA 929-1

13

2
The Excitement of Discovery

THE EARLY COLLECTORS

The first native Canadian plants began arriving in Europe in the sixteenth century aboard ships carrying explorers home from their daring adventures in the New World. By this time, the great Age of Exploration was underway, and explorers sent to find new lands to the east and west often returned home with other new discoveries, including plant species that Europeans had never seen before.

These new plant discoveries caused considerable excitement back home where there was already an intense interest in botany and a fascination with plants and flowers. By the early decades of the seventeenth century, John Tradescant the Elder had brought home new and exotic plants from Russia and the Middle East to his famous gardens at Hatfield House and Oatlands.

This was also the time when plants were first studied under a microscope, and plant reproduction and hybridization began to be understood. These scientific advances only increased the public's interest. Botanical gardens such as those at Chelsea and Kew in England became favourite places for outings, and the collecting of botanical prints, drawings, illustrated botanical books and *hortus siccus* (mounted dried plants) became fashionable pursuits. This excitement about the cultivation of new plants was so notable that some writers have referred to what was happening by the seventeenth and eighteenth centuries as a "gardening revolution." As Keith Thomas points out in *Man and the Natural World*, "In 1500 there were

An illustration from Catharine Parr Traill's classic *Canadian Wild Flowers*, a large format publication with one- or two-page descriptions of each plant. The hand-tinted lithographs are by her niece Agnes Fitzgibbon, the daughter of famous pioneer writer Susanna Moodie, who was Traill's sister.

Catherine Parr Traill, *Canadian Wild Flowers*, illustrations by Agnes Fitzgibbon (Montreal: Lovell, 1868), unpaginated/National Library of Canada

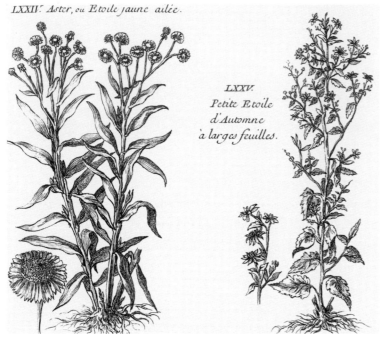

These asters are a good example of the ninety-eight line drawings of North American plants and trees included in the eighteenth-century record of Pierre-François de Charlevois's journey to New France.

Pierre-François de Charlevois, *Histoire et description générale de la Nouvelle France: avec le Journal historique d'un voyage fait par ordre du Roi ... Tome II.* (Paris: Rolin fils, 1744), opposite 42/National Library of Canada 22214

perhaps 200 kinds of cultivated plant in England ... in 1839 the figure was put at 18,000."[1]

Most of the early studies of plant life in Canada were undertaken in the eighteenth and beginning of the nineteenth centuries by explorers, apothecaries and priests. Explorers eagerly recorded everything new they came across. As they treated the diseases and wounds of early settlers, apothecaries studied and catalogued native medicinal plants. And the botanist priests of New France left an astonishing legacy of works that helped define the natural history of Quebec.

It was no accident that a gardening revolution coincided with the Age of Exploration. The early explorers were sent not only to discover new lands but also to collect information on minerals, animals and plants—anything they thought might be of value to the sponsors who funded their voyages. They recorded descriptions of their findings in diaries and journals. These often included sketches and paintings because there was usually at least one artist in the party whose tasks included the recording of animal and plant life. The reports of these early explorers and travellers were among the first descriptions of North American plants to arrive in Europe. Although none could be formally defined as flora—the systematic description of the plant life of a particular region—detailed descriptions and drawings of native

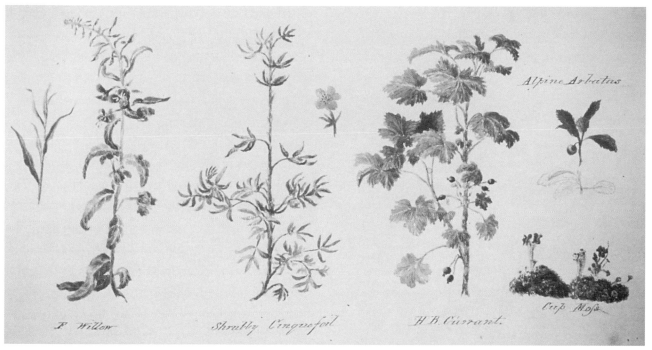

Alpine Arbutus

Cup Moss

F. Willow

Shrubby Cinquefoil

H.B. Currant.

George Back was an Arctic explorer and one of the most important recorders of life in the Canadian Arctic in the early decades of the nineteenth century. He accompanied Franklin to the Coppermine River in 1819. These botanical sketches, in watercolour over pencil, were made while travelling on the Mackenzie River near Great Bear Lake.

National Archives of Canada C-093027

plants were frequently appended to diaries and journals of a voyage of exploration. These became a source for later flora.

Many of the early European explorers carried plant material and seeds back and forth between the continents. From his voyages to the Americas as early as the 1490s, Christopher Columbus was introducing

such things as tobacco, potatoes and corn to Europe. On return trips his ships carried grain back to the New World, the continuation of a long tradition of establishing trade in edible plants everywhere people travelled. Trees and other plants often made the long voyage across the Atlantic. Jacques Cartier is said to have introduced Canadian white pine (*Pinus strobus*)

17

One of the earliest reports of the growing conditions on the east coast of Canada is included in the record of a voyage of Sir Humphrey Gilbert, who arrived in Newfoundland on a colonizing venture from England in 1583:

> The soil along the coast is not deep of earth bringing forth abundantly peas, small yet good feeding for cattle. Roses passing sweet, like unto our musk roses in form, raspberries, a berry we call worts, good and wholesome to eat ... Peas which our countrymen have sown in the time of May have come up fair, and been gathered in the beginning of August ... being the first fruits coming up by art and industry in that desolate and dishabited land.[2]

and eastern white cedar (*Thuja occidentalis*) to Europe in the 1530s.

The first dedicated study of North American native plants was undertaken by the Jesuit missionaries in New France, who were encouraged as part of their duties to collect native plants and test them in holding gardens until they could be sent back to France. Many of these ended up in Paris in the famous Jardin des Plantes (originally Jardin du Roi) where plants from all over the world were cultivated during the seventeenth century. Many of the plants whose botanical names now include "*canadensis*" or "*canadense*" were first recorded by the Jesuits, as in our native columbine (*Aquilegia canadensis*) and bloodroot (*Sanguinaria canadensis*).

On the west coast of Canada, Spanish and English explorers were the most important collectors of botanical information, although much of their original work has been lost. By the late eighteenth century, Spanish naturalists were collecting plants along the coast of British Columbia, often in ships captained by men who left their names behind as reminders of their visits (Malaspina, Quadra and Alberni are a few examples). The Royal Botanical Garden established by the Spanish in Mexico City in 1787 included plant collections from these explorations. In her interesting summary of this period in *Plantae Occidentalis: 200 Years of Botanical Art in British Columbia*, Maria Newberry House explains that political intrigue, the Napoleonic invasions and Spain's well-recognized reputation for secrecy meant that the work of the early botanists along Canada's west coast did not receive the recognition it deserved.

During the first half of the 1790s, Captain George Vancouver set out to explore the west coast of North America. Archibald Menzies, a Scot, accompanied him as surgeon and naturalist. Menzies made numerous botanical discoveries at Nootka and along the coast of British Columbia, and his descriptions of these were later included in Sir W.J. Hooker's *Flora Boreali-Americana*. But Menzies, too, failed to receive proper credit for his discoveries.

Early plant collectors in North America had a difficult time of it. With few if any roads, their travel was by foot or canoe. But these were intrepid adventurers, braving discomfort and danger to gather yet

In 1753 the Swedish botanist Carl Linnaeus published *Species Plantarum*, in which he used his new binomial system for classifying and naming the plants. In the Linnaean system, each plant species is assigned to a genus (a collection of closely related species) and given a Latin name (for the genus) with an accompanying descriptive adjective (for the species). *Species Plantarum* became a standard reference work, and the system of naming plants developed by Linnaeus remains the basis of modern botany. Before this, plant names often included a long Latin description. Latin continues to be used for the scientific names of plants so that no matter what language a scientist or gardener uses, plant names can be recognized by all.

In the Heritage Garden at VanDusen Botanical Garden is this reproduction of the Menzies Frame, a structure used for growing plants on board the *Discovery*, Captain Vancouver's ship on his epic voyage in 1792. In this frame is a selection of some of the plants that the ship's botanist, Archibald Menzies, discovered.

VanDusen Botanical Garden/Photograph by R. Forster

more new species. Finding the new plants wasn't even half the battle. The paper needed for drying the plants was scarce. Unscrupulous collectors stole specimens. Plants were lost. Manuscripts were destroyed by fire. Sometimes sponsors of a trip died or withdrew their support.

When collectors arrived back in a settled area, the difficulties continued. They had to carefully package and ship specimens of the new plants back to Europe as quickly as possible, in the hope of being first with that particular species—and perhaps having it named for the collector! (Plant hunters seemed to think that plants had no names until they were discovered and named by Europeans.) Even if they packaged their plants with great care, shipments were often seriously damaged or lost at sea. Stories of the early North American naturalists are filled with physical distress and danger, competition and intrigue, and disappointing losses. The naturalist-explorers accepted these and other difficulties for a variety of reasons, some in the hope of making a profit, some out of scientific dedication, most for the sheer love of adventure.

Among these early plant collectors was André Michaux, a French botanist and explorer who travelled in Europe, Persia and the United States. In 1792 he canoed through unexplored territory up the Saguenay River. During his lifetime, Michaux assembled a large herbarium. He was particularly interested in trees and introduced a number of Canadian species to Europe. His book *Flora boreali-Americana*, published after his death, created the pattern for the flora that came after.

Throughout the century, Europeans were introduced to the beauty of North American wildflowers and to exciting new vegetables from the Americas. Even the Jerusalem artichoke, a North American member of the sunflower family, became a fashionable vegetable in Europe for a time.

EARLY CANADIAN FLORA

The first book devoted to the subject of plant life in Canada was published in 1635. *Canadensium Plantarum Historia* was written in Latin by Jacques-Philippe Cornut, a Parisian physician who had never set foot in Canada. Its illustrations were probably based on the plants in the famous Jardin des Plantes and on descriptions brought back by explorers and other travellers. It is believed that much of the information and the examples he relied on were sent to the Jardin des Plantes by the pioneer apothecary Louis Hébert, whose life in Canada is described in chapter 3.

Michel Sarrazin was the first person to begin a serious catalogue of the native plants of New France. Sarrazin came to Quebec City in 1685 as a surgeon-

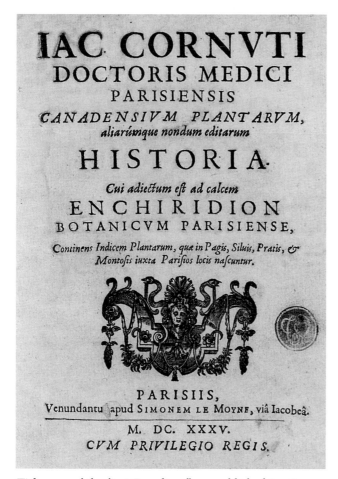

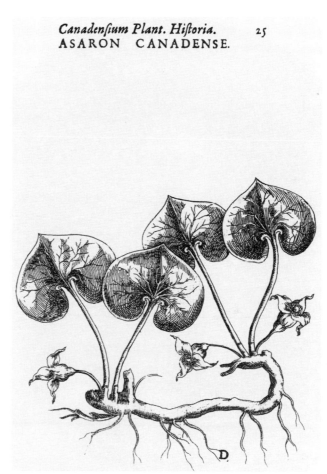

Title page of the first Canadian flora, published in 1635 and based on native Canadian plants found in the famous Jardin des Plantes in Paris. In the preface, Cornut pays tribute to an unnamed explorer, possibly Samuel de Champlain, who sent back botanical information and samples from his voyages in Canada.

This illustration of wild ginger (*Asarum canadense*), which grows in the woods of eastern Canada, is one of thirty-eight illustrations in Jacques-Philippe Cornut's *Canadensium Plantarum Historia*. The name of the artist is unknown.

Jacques-Philippe Cornut, *Canadensium Plantarum Historia* (Paris: Venundantur apud Simonem Le Moyne, 1635)/National Library of Canada 22218-9

Michel Sarrazin

general to the colonial troops and was appointed *médecin du roi* (king's physician) in 1697. Before his appointment, he spent three years back in France where he was a frequent visitor to the Jardin des Plantes (the future Musée d'Histoire Naturelle). Keenly interested in all of nature, Sarrazin spent the next thirty years in New France collecting minerals, describing the animals and contributing seeds and plants to the Jardin des Plantes. His own herbarium (a collection of mounted plants) is said to have included almost 800 specimens. He later collaborated with the French botanist Sébastien Vaillant on a manuscript entitled *L'Histoire des plantes de Canada*.

It was Sarrazin's successor as *médecin du roi* in New France, Jean-François Gaultier, who guided Swedish botanist Pehr Kalm on his collecting excursions there in 1749. Kalm had been sent to North America by the Swedish Academy of Sciences. His assignment in New France was part of a project to find seeds of plants and trees that grew in northern regions and that might be useful in Sweden. Kalm's research was published in three volumes and in a number of scientific journals, and was widely translated. It included a special study of the uses of the maple tree in Canada. Tragically, his manuscript on the flora of Canada was destroyed by fire before it could be published.

Kalm obviously enjoyed his time in New France. He was a man who took an interest in everything—the weather, marriage customs, the remedy for bed-bugs and even how to make sauerkraut. He greatly admired the inhabitants of New France, who had wel-comed him into their homes. They are, he wrote, "more civilized and clever than in any other place of the world that I have visited."[3] To thank Jean-François Gaultier for his help as a guide, Kalm named the win-tergreen plant, *Gaultheria procumbens*, in his honour.

Frederick Pursh was the most important botanist working in North America in the early part of the nine-teenth century. His *Flora Americae Septentrionalis*, published in 1814, became the standard reference for the continent. After completing it, he settled in Montreal intending to follow up with a major flora on Canada. There he suffered the kind of setback that early botanists experienced with distressing regularity when his collection was destroyed by fire. Heartbroken and in poverty, he died in 1820.

THE BOTANIST PRIESTS OF QUEBEC

During the nineteenth and early twentieth centuries, it was the clergy who contributed most to the study of botany in Quebec. The monasteries and convents of New France produced many of the early botanists, who followed a long tradition of cultivating medici-nal plants in their gardens. The most famous of these botanist priests were Abbé Léon Provancher in the nineteenth century and Frère Marie-Victorin in the twentieth.

Abbé Provancher was born in Trois-Rivières in 1820. From an early age, he took an interest in plants and trees. The first of the nineteenth-century natu-ralists in Quebec, Provancher was highly critical of the lack of appreciation for science within the province. To help improve the situation, he published *Traité élémentaire de botanique* in 1858, the first Canadian botanical textbook published in French. He went on to write *Le Verger canadien*, published in 1862. Provancher later published and wrote most of a magazine devoted to natural history, *Le Naturaliste canadien*.

Provancher's *Flore canadienne* appeared the same year as *Le Verger canadien* and was the first book of its kind published in French in North America. It is full of detailed information about the plant life he

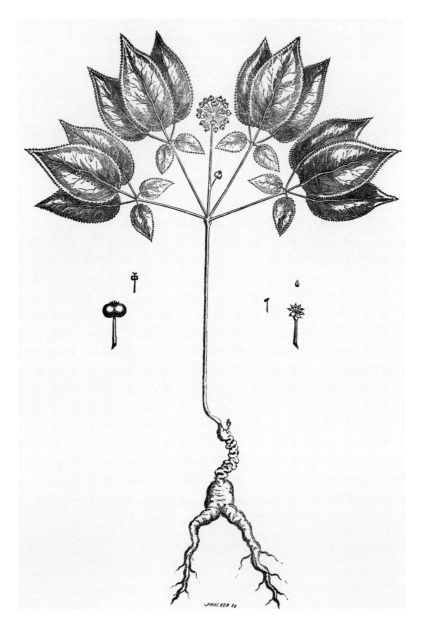

Ginseng (*Panax quinquefolis*), now a nationally protected species in Canada, was once common in eastern deciduous forests. Joseph-François Lafitau recognized it as the medicinal plant popular in China while he was studying the Iroquois near Caughnawauga from 1713 to 1718. Because of its extremely valuable root, the inhabitants were eager to profit from its sale. Unfortunately, it was so badly cured that the Chinese considered it useless. Eventually, over-harvesting almost denuded the landscape of the plants, and it is rarely seen today. The ginseng now exported from Canada (*Panax pseudo ginseng*) is grown commercially. This illustration appeared originally in Lafitau's published report of his discovery.

Joseph-François Lafitau, *Mémoire présenté a Son Altesse Royale Mgr. le duc D'Orléans, régent de France, concernant la précieuse plante du gin-seng ...* (Paris: Mongé, 1718)/National Library of Canada 22217

had studied so carefully. It also included many illustrations from American Asa Gray's *Flora of North America*, and when Gray accused Provancher of plagiarism, his book was discredited. He later gained worldwide recognition for his work as an entomologist when his *Petit faune entomologique du Canada*, describing more than one thousand new insect species, was published. Provancher has been called "Canada's first great teacher of natural history, her first great botanist and a fitting predecessor to Marie-Victorin ... He never wavered from his determination to advance the cause of natural history in Canada, in

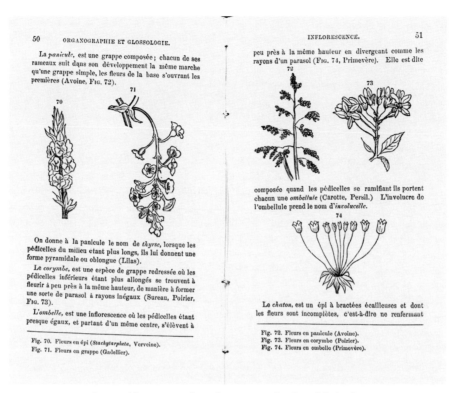

Pages from Abbé Provancher's botany textbook published in 1858.

Abbé Léon Provancher, *Traité élémentaire de botanique* (Quebec: St. Michel et Darveau, 1858)/National Library of Canada 22216

spite of the most difficult circumstances, and he left as his legacy an enormous body of descriptive and narrative publications along with the collections on which his scientific work was based."[4]

A number of other Quebec priests assisted in the development of botanical studies in Canada during the nineteenth century: Abbé Nazaire Leclerc, author of *Le catéchisme d'agriculture*; Abbé Louis-Ovide Brunet, author of *Éléments de botanique et de physiologie végétale*; and Abbé Jean Moyen, who wrote a book for students and amateur botanists. However, it was Frère Marie-Victorin, in the first half of the twentieth century, who made the greatest contribution of all.

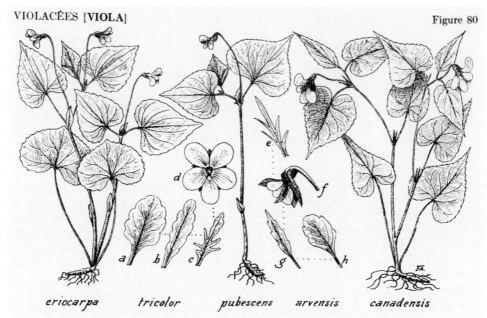

VIOLACÉES [VIOLA]   Figure 80

eriocarpa   tricolor   pubescens   arvensis   canadensis

Viola: *V. eriocarpa*, plante entière; *V. tricolor*, (a–b) feuilles, (c) stipule, (d) fleur; *V. pubescens*, plante en tière; *V. arvensis*, (e) stipule, (f) fleur, (g–h) feuilles; *V. canadensis*, plante entière.

Frère Marie-Victorin, *Flore laurentienne* (Montreal: La Salle, 1935), details 281, 593/National Library of Canada 22204, 22206

FRÈRE MARIE-VICTORIN: QUEBEC'S BELOVED BOTANIST

Frère Marie-Victorin was born Conrad Kirouac in 1885. He grew up in Quebec City, the son of a prosperous merchant. At sixteen he joined the priesthood in Montreal. Frequently ill during these years, he spent much of his convalescence studying plant life. At a time when the botanical knowledge of the province remained relatively undeveloped, he threw himself into collecting specimens, studying the information available and exchanging opinions with others around the world. Although health problems plagued him for most of his life, Marie-Victorin undertook numerous field trips, not only throughout Quebec but around the world, most frequently in Cuba where, for the sake of his deteriorating health, he spent his last years.

Marie-Victorin's interests were broad, and his desire to excite his fellow citizens about the natural

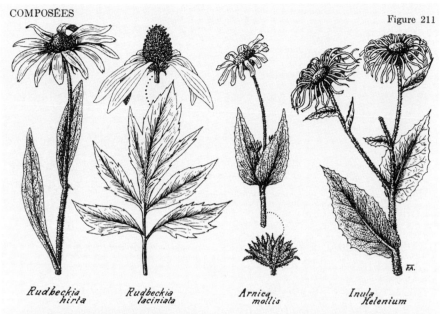

COMPOSÉES   Figure 211

Rudbeckia   Rudbeckia   Arnica   Inula
hirta   laciniata   mollis   Helenium

Rudbeckia: *R. hirta,* sommité florifère; *R. laciniata,* feuille, capitule. — **Arnica:** *A. mollis,* sommité florifère, involucre. — **Inula:** *I. Helenium,* rameau florifère.

world around them made him the centre of intellectual life in Quebec in the early years of the twentieth century. At twenty he had already become an inspiring teacher, a role he excelled at for most of his life. He was the founder of the Botanical Institute of the University of Montreal, where he lectured for years, and was involved in the creation of the Young Naturalists Clubs, the Canadian Society of Natural History and the French-Canadian Association for the Advancement of the Sciences. He spoke passionately on issues of natural science. His public lectures aroused the interest of large audiences, and his work with young people fostered their interest in the sciences. With all of this, Marie-Victorin still found time to write close to a hundred papers on botanical subjects. Finally, in 1935, his magnificent *Flore laurentienne* was published, an impeccable and readable flora on the plants of the Upper St. Lawrence Valley.

The list of Marie-Victorin's accomplishments is an inspiring legacy, which has seldom if ever been matched. His contribution to the intellectual development of Quebec was profound. One of his most significant achievements was the creation of Le Jardin botanique de Montréal. It was he who gained the support of the premier of Quebec, the mayor of Montreal and *Le Devoir* for the undertaking. Appropriately, he is honoured as its founder.

FILLING IN THE PICTURE

Gradually, across the country regional flora were being written, illustrated and published. Catharine Parr Traill, who emigrated from England to Upper Canada (Ontario) in 1832, was a devoted amateur naturalist. Although not educated as a botanist in the formal sense, she was a keen observer and carefully collected and studied the plants of the region around Peterborough over sixty-seven years. Traill, too, was in touch with other experts in the field, and while raising nine children in the backwoods under the most difficult conditions, she managed to produce valuable journal articles and books on the plant life around her.

Traill's accounts are accurate, but also colourful and charming: "On light loamy or sandy soil our gay Lupine may be seen gladdening the wastes and purpling the ground with its long spikes of azure blue, white and purple flowers of many shades."[5] Her view of nature was influenced always by her deep belief in God. In the words of historian Carl Berger:

> Like all romantics, Traill sought not merely to depict what she saw, but to convey her own emotional responses to nature. Hers was the spirit of the immigrant, an exile, living in a strange country where the woods were so astonishingly silent and the months of March and April so desolate ... The cycles of growth and the transitoriness of flowers became for Traill metaphors for human destiny, underlining the fragility of life but also offering proof of a caring providence.[6]

Traill's most famous books, aside from her biographical account of pioneer life in *The Backwoods of Canada*, are the illustrated *Canadian Wild Flowers* and the more ambitious *Studies of Plant Life in Canada*.

As the decades went by, people began to understand the value of the scientific study of plant life. By the 1830s the importance of such studies to agriculture was acknowledged. Two decades later the universities were setting up separate departments of botany. In the 1850s botanical societies began springing up, and interested amateurs were being encouraged to go into the countryside and collect plant specimens.

James Barnston was the moving force behind the

Scottish-born David Douglas was one of the most famous of the North American plant hunters. As a young man in the 1820s, he explored along Lake Erie near Amherstburg, collecting specimens as he went, and later along the Columbia, Okanagan and Fraser rivers. Here he faced the usual dangers and discomfort:

"Circumstances obliged me to leave the ground hastily ... a party of eight Indians endeavoured to destroy me. I returned to the camp, got the horses saddled, and made a speedy retreat. To-day I killed two large bears, and one next morning. With hostile Indians and incessant rains, together with the lateness of the season, fatigued and broken down I could have but little zeal to continue my exertions."[7]

Although he only lived to be thirty-five, Douglas introduced 254 North American plants to Europe (more than anyone before him). He had fifty plants named after him, including the remarkable Douglas fir (*Pseudotsuga menziesii*).

B.C. Archives PDP08716

formation of the Botanical Society of Montreal in 1855. He had been encouraged by George Dawson, the much-honoured director of the Geological Survey of Canada whose interests lay more in the study of palaeobotany. Although only twenty-seven when he died, Barnston made notable contributions to the knowledge of plant life in central Canada. He was especially active in encouraging young people to "botanize"—to collect plant specimens by roaming the countryside. In Kingston in 1860, the Botanical Society of Canada was founded. All those interested in plants were free to join—even Sir John A. Macdonald was a member. Its founder, George Lawson, reported: "We already have observers the length and breadth of Canada, as well as in the other North American Provinces, from the Red River in the far West to the Island of Prince Edward in the East."[8] But there were plenty of problems along the way. As botany developed as a new discipline, scholars began to disagree. As elsewhere in the world, there were heated debates over the conflicts between science and religion, which Charles Darwin had unleashed when his evolutionary ideas were published in *On the Origin of Species* in 1859.

More and more botanists and interested amateurs were combing the fields and forests for new native species. Even in the nineteenth century, however, few of their discoveries were being published in Canada. Though American flora began to include sections on native Canadian plants (Frederick Pursh and André Michaux included 400 Canadian locales in their early works), there was a serious need for a publication devoted to plant life across Canada.

JOHN MACOUN: COLLECTOR EXTRAORDINAIRE

A more formal interest in the country's flora had to wait for government support, which finally came in the 1880s. This next step forward was the result of the obsessions of one man, John Macoun. Collecting plants—and being the first to record new Canadian species—was the most important thing in Macoun's life. But he didn't confine himself to plants. He was a tireless collector of all flora and fauna and the key figure in the establishment of the Victoria Memorial Museum in Ottawa, the country's first national museum.

John Macoun arrived in Canada from Ireland in 1850 at the age of nineteen. He spent the next six years working on his family's farm ninety miles east of Toronto, but his true interest lay in the study of the natural world around him. Macoun chose teaching as a career, which allowed him the freedom to concentrate on collecting plants in the summer. By 1862 he

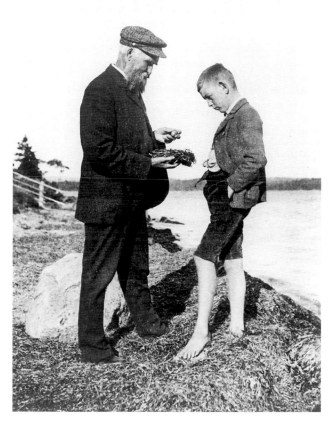

John Macoun was said to have collected more than 100,000 plant specimens, which became the basis of the Dominion Herbarium in Ottawa. He is seen here with a young naturalist in the Maritimes in the 1890s.

National Archives of Canada PA-120487

was married and living and teaching in Belleville. It was here that he created his personal herbarium, which he hoped would one day become a complete collection of all Canadian plant life.

Throughout his lifetime, Macoun was rewarded with a series of important positions—first as a member of the Geological Survey of Canada, then as Dominion Botanist and finally as Naturalist of the Survey. The last two involved considerable administrative work, something that Macoun was never particularly interested in. Despite his office obligations, as soon as spring was in the air Macoun took to the fields and woods. Some of his field trips were harrowing and hazardous. The following excerpt is from his diary of a trip (with one companion) down the Peace River for the Geological Survey in 1875:

> Poor food and hard work now began to tell on me. My stomach loathed raw pemmican, and all other food was gone—our gun was useless—and it became painfully evident that from some unaccountable cause, the boats had not yet left Fort Chipweyan. Sixty miles lay between us and safety, and we must either hurry on or starve. We toiled on until after mid-day, when I became so ill that we had to put ashore. I lay down on the sand utterly exhausted and very sick. A review of the situation brought me to myself, and I rose, determined to struggle on as

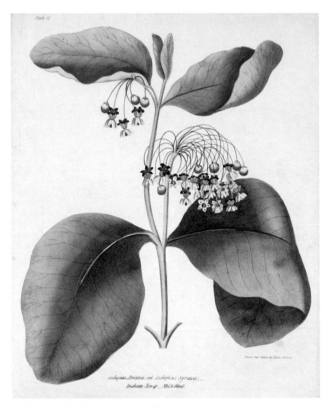

Milkweed (identified as Indian hemp). One of a series of hand-coloured lithographs reproduced from the watercolours of Nova Scotian Maria Morris. Botanist Titus Smith assisted her by finding and identifying the plants of the province. Morris worked on botanical illustration from the 1830s to the 1870s.

Maria Morris, *Wildflowers of Nova Scotia*, botanical information by Titus Smith (Halifax: Belcher, 1840), unpaginated/National Library of Canada

long as I could hold the paddle. Without a word we worked on and on and reached Quatre Fourche River long after dark. Tying the canoe to the bushes we crawled up the bank and were soon asleep.[9]

Canadian botanical discoveries and the naming of new plants were still, for the most part, dependent on records verified and maintained in the United States and England. Many Canadians were beginning to be concerned about this reliance on outside experts who published new findings after Canadians had done the legwork. In the second half of the nineteenth century Canadian journals, such as *Transactions of the Literary and Historical Society of Quebec* and *The Canadian Journal* (published in Toronto), began to include lists of new plants in their pages. Macoun, however, had no compunctions about sending his discoveries to be verified by outside experts. In 1864 one of the sedges he discovered, *Carex macounii*, was named after him by the American expert who verified his find. It was the first of sixty-nine flowering plants, mosses and lichens that Macoun discovered and had named in his honour.

An enthusiastic and energetic collector, Macoun was sometimes criticized for not being careful enough with his identifications and the preservation of his specimens, but he was nonetheless respected for the collections he sent to experts in the United States and England. His crowning achievement was his seven-part *Catalogue of Canadian Plants*, published between 1883 and 1902. It won him the respect of naturalists in Canada and abroad.

Numerous Canadian flora have been published in the twentieth century. Photography has changed the recording of plants in the wild in some ways, but photographs will never replace botanical illustrations and the skill with which artists are able to record and highlight important plant features for identification. There are now popular books to help identify the most common wildflowers, more scientific volumes detailing the less well-known sedges and grasses, broad-ranging works such as H.J. Scoggan's four volume *The Flora of Canada*, individual botanical titles for each of the provinces (including the writings on arctic and subarctic flora by Ernest Lepage and Arthème Dutilly), and more narrowly based studies of special regions and microclimates. Perhaps John Macoun's dream of recording every native Canadian species has finally been realized. ❧

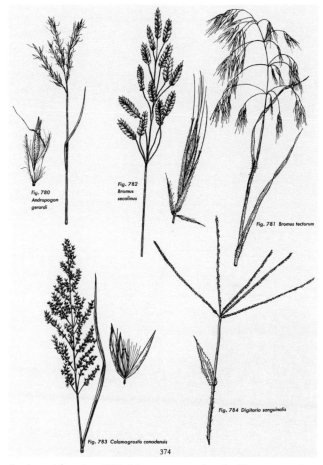

In the mid 1960s, F.H. Montgomery, head of botany at the Ontario Agricultural College, saw the need for an up-to-date national flora—something that would help travellers interested in identifying the plants they found across the country. He carefully organized 1500 plants, keying them to genera and species. Over 870 were illustrated with line drawings.

F.H. Montgomery, *Plants from Sea to Sea* (Toronto: Ryerson, 1966), 374/National Library of Canada 22207

3
Pioneer Gardeners

Early in the seventeenth century when the French arrived on the east coast of Canada planning to establish permanent settlements, cultivating the land was one of their priorities. No settlement could survive without gardens to supply fresh food and medicinal herbs.

The first attempt to create a settlement was at Isle Saint-Croix in 1604-5. Samuel de Champlain accompanied the settlers as mapmaker. When cruel weather and scurvy forced the colonists to leave Saint-Croix and cross the Bay of Fundy to the mainland, they resettled at what Champlain called Port-Royal,

---

The Retreat, a watercolour by Reverend William Arthur Johnson of his father's home in Dunn Township in 1847, shows an orchard to the right of the house and a kitchen garden in front.

Toronto Reference Library/MTL 1312

now Annapolis Royal in Nova Scotia. As cartographer, Champlain not only charted the geography of the country, but also prepared maps of the settlements. In all of these, he included plots for gardens. As we know from his writings, he also took a personal interest in gardening:

> I also did mine [his garden at Saint-Croix], which was fairly big; and in it I sowed a quantity of seeds, as did the others who had any. These came up pretty well, but as the island was nothing but sand, everything was almost burnt when the sun shone; for we had no water with which to water them excepting from rain, and this did not fall often.[1]

In the summer of 1606, more settlers were sent out to Port-Royal from France. Among them was Louis Hébert, a Parisian apothecary. Since it was Hébert's responsibility as apothecary to dispense medicines to the colonists, the cultivation of medicinal herbs was his immediate concern. His gardens in the

35

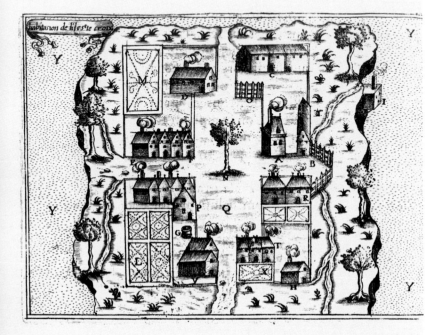

Champlain first attempted to establish a settlement in 1604 at Isle Saint-Croix on the south shore of the Bay of Fundy. This map of the proposed settlement, from a sketch by Champlain, shows the areas set aside for gardens. Although the settlement failed within the year, when some of the settlers returned the following year they found lettuce, sorrel and cabbage still growing among the weeds.

Samuel de Champlain, *Voyages du Sieur de Champlain …* (Paris: Berjon, 1613),38/National Library of Canada 15306

In 1604-5 Samuel de Champlain was a member of the exploration party that travelled as far south as Massachusetts. Here he wrote one of the earliest reports of Native gardening: "We saw their grain, which is Indian corn. This they grow in gardens, sowing three or four grains in one spot, after which, with the shells of the aforesaid signoc [horseshoe crab], they heap about it a quantity of earth. Then three feet away they sow as much again, and so on in order. Amongst this corn they plant in each hillock three or four Brazilian beans, which come up of different colours. When fully grown these plants twine around the aforementioned corn, which grows to a height of five or six feet … We saw there many squashes, pumpkins, and tobacco, which they likewise cultivate."[2]

little settlement of two or three hundred people at Port-Royal were the first European experimental seed plots in North America. The Port-Royal settlement was abandoned in 1607, and Hébert and the other settlers sailed back to France.

In 1608 Champlain was sent back to Canada in another attempt to establish a French colony. He travelled up the St. Lawrence as far as present-day Quebec City, this time as lieutenant to the head of the expedition. Here they established a habitation, or settlement. Champlain again showed his interest in testing the soil by planting a vegetable garden, as well as vines and grains. "As for the country itself," he wrote:

> It is beautiful and agreeable, and it brings all sorts of grains and seeds to maturity. There are in it all the varieties of trees we have in our forests on this side of the ocean and many fruits, although they are wild for lack of cultivation: such as butternut trees, cherry-trees, plum-trees, vines, raspberries, strawberries, gooseberries and red currants, and several other small fruits, which are quite good. There are also several sorts of useful herbs and roots.[3]

In the winter of 1616-17 when Champlain was back in Paris looking for support for the colony, he met Louis Hébert again. He managed to convince Hébert that there was good land and a good income for colonists willing to settle at Quebec. Hébert sold his

Marie Hébert, known as the Mother of Canada, was the wife of Louis Hébert. They are recognized as French Canada's first gardeners. This line drawing is by C.W. Jefferys, the well-known illustrator of Canadian history.

National Archives of Canada/C-006563

house and garden, and with his wife, Marie Rollet, and their three children, he set sail for New France. The family arrived at Quebec in the spring of 1617 determined to make the best of it, in spite of the difficulties put in their way by the trading company. Tensions between the settlers and the fur traders plagued the early settlements. Although the traders welcomed the supplies that such centres could provide, they were well aware that as settlers cleared and planted the land, the animals on which their livelihood depended would be forced farther and farther into the interior. This conflict between the needs of settled populations and the desire to preserve nature has continued to be a factor in Canadian life.

The Héberts managed to clear their twenty arpents of land (about eight hectares), which was located high on the cliff overlooking Quebec. In his journals, Champlain described visiting the Héberts' flourishing garden in 1618. By 1626 the Héberts had been granted additional land and were cultivating

> grain fields, vegetable gardens, and an orchard planted with apple trees brought from Normandy. All this had been achieved in spite of the company's opposition. Moreover, it had been accomplished with hand-tools only, not even a plough.[4]

Establishing an apple orchard was an important early undertaking for the settlers because cider was the main beverage at the time. As early as 1621 Champlain had planted the first Normandy apple tree on the heights of Quebec City. He left Hébert to tend the apple trees to ensure they survived and became acclimatized to the harsh weather of New France.

The Héberts have gone down in history as the first farmers of New France. But Louis Hébert was more than a gardener and farmer. Many believe that it was Hébert who provided the descriptions and plants for Jacques-Philippe Cornut's 1635 *Canadensium Plantarum Historia*, described in chapter 2.

Champlain is justly loved and admired for his bravery in exploration and his skill as a cartographer. His detailed journals brought him fame and recognition and left us a record of some of the earliest European attempts at gardening in New France.

Jean Talon, the powerful Intendant of the colony in the 1660s, encouraged farming and initiated trade in flax and hemp with the West Indies. He established a model farm of his own as an example to the settlers. There, among his other crops, he grew fields of hops, valuable not only for making beer but also as the leavening agent used for making bread. Hops remained an important crop for almost two hundred years. In *Historic Canadian Ground*, published in 1882, John Fraser wrote: "Very few of the present generation would hardly realize that over sixty years ago there was a farm within eight miles of Montreal having seventy acres of hops growing in it."[5] Naturalized hop plants can still be found growing on what were once pioneer fields.

Throughout the seventeenth century, the production of food was the basis of the economy of the settlements. The major crop by far was wheat, essential

Hop pickers in 1902 at Bloomfield in Prince Edward County, Ontario, when hops were still an important crop.

Archives of Ontario/C130-1-0-3-5

for bread, but the tithing records of the churches of New France show the importance of potatoes and corn as well. In each household, women cultivated a *jardin potager*, a small enclosed space used exclusively for growing fruit and vegetables for the family's table. Later, when produce from the home garden was more abundant, families sold it in markets that sprang up in village squares. For the early colonists of New France, gardening for the sake of beauty was a luxury they could not afford.

Pehr Kalm, the Swedish naturalist who visited the colony in 1749, described the vegetables growing in a *jardin potager* in Quebec City:

> Kitchen herbs succeed very well here. White cabbage is very fine but sometimes suffers greatly from worms. Onions (*Allium cepa*) are very much in use here together with other species of leeks. They likewise plant several species of pumpkins, melons, lettuce, wild chiccory or wild endive (*Cichorium intybus*), several kinds of peas, beans, Turkish beans, carrots, and cucumbers. They have plenty of red beets, horseradish, and common radishes, thyme, and marjoram. Turnips are sown in abundance and used chiefly in winter. Parsnips are sometimes eaten, though not very commonly. Few people took notice of potatoes, and neither the common (*Solanum tuberosum*) nor the Bermuda ones (*Convulvulus batatas*) were planted in Canada; only a few had any

artichokes. When the French here are asked why they do not plant potatoes, they answer that they do not like them and they laugh at the English who are so fond of them.[6]

While travelling from Montreal to Quebec by boat, Kalm noted:

> Every farmer plants a quantity of tobacco near his house, in proportion to the size of his family. It is necessary that one should plant tobacco because it is so universally smoked by the common people. Boys of ten or twelve years of age, as well as the old people, run about with a pipe in their mouth.[7]

LOUISBOURG

In 1713 when the Treaty of Utrecht put Acadia in the hands of Britain, many of the French Acadians started a new home in Louisbourg, which became the capital of Île Royale (now Cape Breton). Although the colony's economy depended almost solely on the export of cod, the Acadians grew as much food as they could. There were more than a hundred gardens within the walls of Louisbourg's fortress. Seeds were brought over from France, and a census of Île Royale in 1752 lists cabbages, turnips, beans, peas, pumpkins and root crops growing on the island.

The gardens of the leading citizens of Louisbourg

In the reconstruction of Louisbourg, undertaken in 1961, great care was taken to recreate the gardens as they originally existed. Here the garden of Étienne Verrier, Chief Engineer of Louisbourg, reflects his important role in the fortress. Its symmetry and luxurious layout is a reflection of the principles laid down in France, while the garden's vegetables, herbs and medicinal plants recognize the need for utility.

Parks Canada, Fortress of Louisbourg/05 K 09 D 701

In the Louisbourg garden of Captain DeGannes, a more utilitarian approach has been taken, with little waste of space. But here, too, the principles of balance and design are honoured. Many herbs and other medicinal plants were grown in the garden, including angelica. Valued for its many medical uses, it was imported and widely grown. It is now considered a noxious weed in Cape Breton.

Parks Canada, Fortress of Louisbourg/05 K 09 D 882

sometimes went beyond the utilitarian. They had neither the means nor the ability to recreate the magnificent gardens of France, but their gardens showed the influence of contemporary French design. French garden style of this period was based on rigidly controlled planting patterns, with symmetrical designs relieved by the careful contrast in colour and texture of the plantings within the design. This aesthetic was epitomized by the famous gardens of Versailles—the pride of Louis XIV.

THE ANNAPOLIS VALLEY

Having seized the rest of the eastern region, Britain was eager to establish colonies. English, German, Irish and Scottish settlers began arriving in 1760. The cultivation of potatoes arrived with them.

In the Annapolis basin, the French Acadians had been dyking the marshland and growing vegetables, flax and wheat for years. In the 1750s and 1760s, Britain expelled them from their land and then enticed New Englanders north with promises of good cleared land. Without the Acadians' skill controlling the dykes, however, the land came to be used for pasture and hay.

From all these settlers, Britain required that they include two acres of hemp as part of their yearly crops. The hemp was sent back to Britain and was used to manufacture the rope and rigging that the navy needed for its ships.

IN THE NORTH

While the French were colonizing the south early in the seventeenth century, Britain was creating settlements in the north through the explorations of the Hudson's Bay Company. For the century following 1670, Britain maintained trading forts around Hudson Bay. Back in England the directors of the company were eager to see these communities become self-sufficient, which included cultivating gardens. Unfortunately, the directors had no idea about the harsh growing conditions these settlers faced. They believed that regions at the same latitude as those at home would have similar climates. Fort Albany (on James Bay), for instance, wasn't far north of London, and Fort York (on Hudson Bay) was about at the latitude of central Scotland. However, the realities of growing significant crops around Hudson Bay were vastly different. Every year the directors optimistically sent the settlers grains and garden seeds and urged the governors to relieve the company

from the great expence we have been att in sending provissions into the Countrey which we beleeve may be done if you appley your selfe to trey in all

42

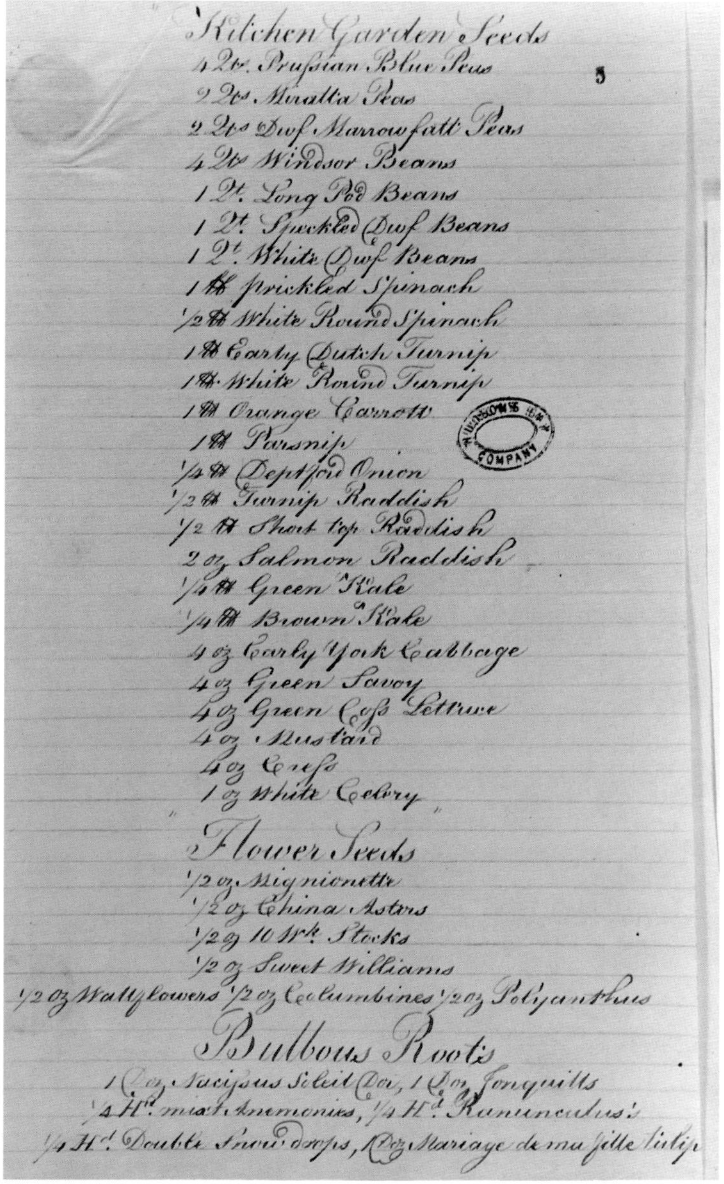

Kitchen Garden Seeds

3

4 lb. Prussian Blue Peas
2 lbs. Miralta Peas
2 lbs. Dwf. Marrowfatt Peas
4 lb. Windsor Beans
1 lb. Long Pod Beans
1 lb. Speckled Dwf. Beans
1 lb. White Dwf. Beans
1 lb. Prickled Spinach
½ lb. White Round Spinach
1 lb. Early Dutch Turnip
1 lb. White Round Turnip
1 lb. Orange Carrott
1 lb. Parsnip
¼ lb. Deptford Onion
½ lb. Turnip Raddish
½ lb. Short top Raddish
2 oz. Salmon Raddish
¼ lb. Green Kale
¼ lb. Brown Kale
4 oz. Early York Cabbage
4 oz. Green Savoy
4 oz. Green Cos Lettuce
4 oz. Mustard
4 oz. Cress
1 oz. White Celery

Flower Seeds

½ oz. Mignionette
½ oz. China Asters
½ oz. 10 Wk. Stocks
½ oz. Sweet Williams
½ oz. Wallflowers ½ oz. Columbines ½ oz. Polyanthus

Bulbous Roots

1 Doz. Nacissus Sileil Dea, 1 Doz. Jonquills
½ Hd. mixt Anemonies, ¼ Hd. Ranunculus's
¼ Hd. Double Snow drops, 1 Doz. Mariage de ma fille Tulips

places were we ar settled what the earth will bring forth & that you may make the experiments we have furnished, you wth. severall sorts of seeds and graynes & will continue to doe soe from yeare to yeare & shall thinke it a very meritorious worke if you effectually prosecute it.[8]

There are few records of the fort gardens in the north, but William Wales, an astronomer who visited Fort Churchill in 1768, reported that dandelions "made most excellent sallad to our roast geese."[9] Already this prolific immigrant to the New World had become well known!

Seeds for the kitchen garden as listed in the Fort Churchill Journal of 1803. The men who directed the Hudson's Bay Company maintained their unrealistic expectations that northern forts could supply more of their own food.

Hudson's Bay Company Archives, Provincial Archives of Manitoba, HBCA B.42/d/81 fo.5 (N14318)

In the early nineteenth century, Patrick Campbell toured the Acadian coutryside, by now in the hands of the English. In this charming, whimsical picture Campbell (he is the one in the hat) shows the stumps still standing in the fields, as they did for many years. The four kinds of fences he saw during his travels, "Virginia rail, worm, log and post-and rails," are all included.

New Brunswick Museum, Saint John, N.B.

THE LOYALISTS

The 1780s marked the beginning of a transformation in the Canadian colonies. Until then the English population was small and French Canadians were by far in the majority. With the end of the American Revolution, 50,000 immigrants loyal to the British Crown moved into the Canadian colonies.

Nova Scotia (including what is now New Brunswick), with a population of only 20,000, was inundated by about 35,000 Loyalist refugees. Distribution of land, supplies and rations became an immediate and overwhelming problem. Free grants of land were speedily awarded, as well as supplies of food and the basic tools required to clear the land and build homes—axes, saws, hoes and spades. All this activity was a powerful stimulus to the economy of the little colony. Most of the refugees were accustomed to city life and cultivated land, so they must have been ill-prepared when they headed off into the Canadian wilderness.

Many who crossed into Quebec found that much of the land was already settled. They continued up the St. Lawrence to Ontario. There they found fertile soil and were encouraged to clear land for farms and gardens along the north shore of the St. Lawrence and Lake Ontario. By the 1780s, 10,000 Loyalists had arrived.

The largest settlement was at Cataraqui (Kingston). Many Loyalists also settled in Prince Edward County to the west, where "in and around the tree stumps they planted the government's gift of grain, the turnip seed, Indian corn, kale and pumpkin that formed most of their diet for years."[10] But food, clothing and tools were all in short supply. When government rations came to an end, many were unable to support themselves, and the two years from 1787 to 1789 became know as the "hungry years." Strangely, vegetables were rarely grown by the settlers during this period. Their diet consisted chiefly of such things as pork (often salted), cornmeal porridge and food from the wild: game, fish, rice, forest greens and berries. The Loyalists who continued on to the Niagara region found a particularly welcoming land and climate. Peach and cherry trees were already being cultivated there by 1793.

Disaffected Americans continued to find their way north, including Mennonites who immigrated to western Ontario and the Niagara region in the 1790s. Skilled and experienced farmers, the Mennonites looked for land that showed its fertility by the kind and size of the trees it supported. Hardwoods were best, especially black walnut. In fact, the Mennonites described their trek as "the trail of the Black Walnut." Next came maple, beech and cherry. In Europe, Mennonites "had been the first to introduce such

James Peachey was an officer assigned to the business of surveying land and settling the Loyalists. Many of his watercolours illustrate this period. This scene, probably near Niagara-on-the-Lake, was painted either in 1783 or 1788-89. Loyalist settlers at Niagara were successful from as early as 1782: "There were then seventeen families farming at Niagara, a total of eighty-four people." Peachey noted that they had cleared an impressive 236 acres and raised 926 bushels of Indian corn and 630 bushels of potatoes.

National Archives of Canada/C-002035

practices as crop rotation, use of animal manure and lime for fertilizers, and legumes to enrich the soil."[11] Using the same practices in Canada, they created farms that were models of industry and success.

When Lower Canada (Quebec) and Upper Canada (Ontario) were created in 1791, both provinces were well on the way to developing a prosperous society of farmers, landowners and merchants.

NINETEENTH-CENTURY UPPER CANADA

One remarkable family has contributed much to our knowledge of pioneer life in Upper Canada during the nineteenth century. Samuel Strickland and his sisters, Catharine Parr Traill and Susanna Moodie, emigrated to Canada from England in the early decades of the century. They reacted to the new country and the life they found here quite differently, but all three left lively accounts of the people, the hardships and the triumphs of life in the bush and the clearing. Samuel and Catharine, in particular, wrote to advise future settlers on what they would find in the Canadas and how best to prepare themselves for this new way of life. Susanna, although she came to appreciate her new life in Canada after leaving the backwoods, professed to be more interested in discouraging would-be settlers: "If these sketches should prove the means of deterring one fam-

ily from sinking their property, and shipwrecking all their hopes, by going to reside in the backwoods of Canada, I shall consider myself amply repaid ..."[12]

Samuel Strickland detailed much of what day-to-day life was like in Canada West (as Upper Canada was renamed in 1841) in his book *Twenty-seven Years in Canada West; or, the Experiences of an Early Settler*. It was Catharine, however, particularly in *The Backwoods of Canada* and *The Female Emigrant's Guide* (later reprinted as *The Canadian Settler's Guide*), who left us the clearest picture of what it was like to tramp through the bush north of Lake Ontario and there create a life and a home from scratch.

In addition to her valuable records on plant life in the woods and fields around her, Catharine described in detail the early cultivation of her garden. During the first year, 1833, she and her husband grew only oats, corn, pumpkins, potatoes and turnips. They had few implements, chiefly a spade and hoe, as well as reaping hooks and "a queer sort of harrow." Wild strawberries and raspberries were moved into their cultivated garden, and native plants, such as cress, wild rice and lamb's quarters, were harvested for the table.

Within two years the Traills had about ten hectares cleared. In addition to grain, they were growing peas, a great variety of beans, lettuces, cabbages and root crops. Catharine was amazed at how quickly the vegetables matured in what seemed such a short growing season. She also extolled the virtues of a root cellar for storing vegetables in the winter months but acknowledged that with so much else to be done, it often took two or three years for new settlers to find the time to construct one.

In the fall of 1834, Catharine wrote that their potato crop had failed because of a drought, but

> [o]ur Indian-corn was very fine; so were our pumpkins. We had some fine vegetables in the garden, especially the peas and melons; the latter were very large and fine. The cultivation of the melon is very simple: you first draw the surrounding earth together with a broad hoe into a heap; the middle of this heap is then slightly hollowed out so as to form a basin, the mould being raised round the edges; into this hollow you insert several melon-seeds, and leave the rest to the summer heat.[13]

The following year Catharine reported that at last the Traills had a proper garden:

> We are having the garden, which hitherto has been nothing but a square enclosure for vegetables, laid out in a prettier form; two half circular wings sweep off from the entrance to each side of the house; the fence is a sort of rude basket or hurdle-work, such as you see at home, called by the country folk wattled fence: this forms a much more picturesque fence than those usually put up of split timber.[14]

The literary family of Samuel Strickland, Catharine Parr Traill and Susanna Moodie left a rich record of life in Upper Canada (later Canada West and now Ontario). They first settled in the Peterborough area, around Lakefield. Although Susanna later moved to Belleville, it is in Peterborough and Lakefield that the family is best remembered and honoured. This historical plaque stands near the Lakefield locks, a few steps from the house in which Catharine lived for nearly half a century.

Photograph by Michael Solomon

"The Canadians call these verandahs 'stoups.' Few
houses, either log or frame, are without them," Catharine
Parr Traill wrote. "The pillars look extremely pretty,
wreathed with the luxuriant hop-vine, mixed with the
scarlet creeper and '*morning glory*,' (the American name
for the most splendid of major convolvuluses)."[15]

W.H. Bartlett, *Canadian Scenery*, illustrated, vol. II (London: Virtue, undated;
facsimile edition, Toronto: Peter Martin, 1967), opposite 23.

Her brother Samuel provided the best descriptions of the important job of establishing an apple orchard:

> I should advise the emigrant, who becomes an agriculturalist, to pay great attention to orchard planting, and, indeed, to devote a portion of his first-cleared fallow for that purpose. The trees should be planted in rows four square rods apart, so that, look at them whichever way you please, they will present a straight row. By this method you will be able to work the land well with the plough, which is essential to the well doing of your orchard.
>
> The young trees should be washed with hot-lime wash, or scrubbed with strong wood-ash lye, or soft-soap, every two or three years, which will prevent canker, and keep the bark bright and clean. Instead of clay for grafting, it is better to use a composition made of bee's-wax, rosin, and grease, put on hot with a brush ... I do not know any thing that gives a greater air of comfort to a farm, than a well-loaded orchard.[16]

OPENING THE WEST

While settlers were developing gardens and farms in the east, the prairies were still mostly open grass-lands where Native hunters and fur traders roamed. Gardening and farming required a much more settled life than the hunters and traders followed. One exception was Peter Pond, a North West Company trader. When Alexander Mackenzie arrived at Pond's post on the Athabasca River in 1788, he found "as fine a kitchen garden as I ever saw in Canada."[17] There Pond was growing turnips, carrots and parsnips, as well as experimenting with potatoes and cabbages.

Where the climate and the land were more conducive to gardening, the fort gardens were much more successful. At the Pembina River post, south of where Winnipeg now stands, Alexander Henry the Younger of the Nor'Westers proudly reported his 1803 harvest:

> I took my vegetables up—300 large heads of cabbage, 8 bushels of carrots, 16 bushels of onions, 10 bushels of turnips, some beets, parsnips, etc. ... potatoes—420 bushels ... I measured an onion, 22 inches in circumference; a carrot, 18 inches long, and, at the thick end, 14 inches in circumference; a turnip with its leaves weighed 25 pounds ...[18]

But it wasn't until 1812, when Lord Thomas Douglas Selkirk led a group of Highlanders to establish the Red River Colony at what is now Winnipeg, that settlement gardens were undertaken. Although the land was rich, the colony failed to flourish in the early years. For one thing, the Scottish crofters were more familiar with raising sheep than with growing produce. Their crops suffered from locusts, floods,

Menno Moyer and his family in Redvers, Saskatchewan, with their produce proudly displayed in front of their sod and lumber home, about 1900.

Saskatchewan Archives Board, Regina R-A 7555

droughts and early frosts. And the fur traders here too were fighting for control of the region, fearing that settlements would destroy their way of life. The settlers who stuck it out, however, were eventually well repaid: "Though the settlers' farming methods remained fairly crude—they still used some wooden ploughs in the 1820s, still sowed the oats and winter

50

wheat by hand, threshed with flails—the crops could be gloriously abundant if natural calamity held off."[19]

In 1858 explorer and naturalist Henry Youle Hind headed a Hudson's Bay Company expedition to the Assiniboine and Saskatchewan rivers. He reported on the gardening successes of the Gowler family farm on the Assiniboine where about twenty hectares were

The MacLaverty family, near Battleford, Saskatchewan, about 1905. In most pioneer families, the women and children were responsible for growing the family's food.

Saskatchewan Archives Board, Donaghy Papers, Regina S-A42

The first home of Susan Allison near Hope, British Columbia. Her family moved into the log house in the 1860s. In her journal she wrote of some of the hazards faced by pioneering gardeners: "We soon had a garden fenced with willow poles and in the open we were foolish enough to plant carrots, potatoes and oats—I say foolish because as soon as the carrots grew to be any size the Black Bears came at night and dug them up and ate them."[20]

B.C. Archives/D 08227

under cultivation. The family's main problem was finding a ready market for what Hind reported were magnificent crops, including potatoes, onions, melons, tobacco and Indian corn.

Towards the end of the nineteenth century, the Mennonite farmers' appreciation of the freedom of the frontier attracted them farther west. The first settlers arrived in Manitoba in 1874, and from there they travelled to British Columbia. "One of the first tasks the settlers had undertaken after their arrival was the planting of thousands of trees—maple, poplar, cottonwood—both as windbreaks and for decoration ... it suited their new prairie villages splendidly."[21]

Daniel Williams Harmon, a New Englander who joined the North West Company in 1800, kept a diary of his experiences working for the company until 1819. It is a fascinating document and of special interest for his gardening records. He lived in various forts across Canada, establishing gardens at every opportunity. In May 1811 at Stuart Lake, New Caledonia, he wrote: "All hands busily employed in clearing away the rubbish from a piece of Ground for a Garden." On May 22, he noted: "Planted our Potatoes & sewed Barley & Turnip Seeds &c." This was probably the first time Europeans cultivated vegetables on the mainland west of the Rocky Mountains.[22]

But even a hundred years later not every prairie settler was growing food for the table. Although potatoes and turnips were basic, according to W.W. Thomson in his history of gardening in Saskatchewan, "few of our people have realized the value of the Kitchen Garden and its inherent possibilities under our conditions. Nothing will add more to the comfort of the home and the beauty of its surroundings than a properly planned and well-tilled garden."[23] Thomson recommended cottonwood, willow or Russian poplar for windbreaks and advocated planting native fruit, such as chokecherries and Saskatoon berries.

Farther west it took the Fraser River gold rush of 1858 in British Columbia to increase the settled population. In 1849, in keeping with its agreement with the British government, the Hudson's Bay Company brought settlers from Great Britain to farm the land. From their farms and gardens, they provided food for the company's men.

The pioneering era of gardening in Canada has never really ended. A few hardy individuals and families continue to carve homes and gardens out of the wilderness north of the narrow band of settlement across the country. They face similar challenges to those of previous centuries. They still cut down the forests, till virgin soil and plant flowers and vegetables where they've never grown before—albeit with more modern equipment and broader access to seeds. And they continue to feel a kinship with those settlers who faced the frontier before them. ❧

4
Settling In

❧

ELEGANT GARDENS OF THE NINETEENTH CENTURY

The generation that followed the pioneering gardeners were more comfortably established than their predecessors. Already by the eighteenth century, the estates of the wealthy residents of Quebec, notably the merchants, had extensive gardens frequently based on those they had seen in Europe. The population of Quebec City had grown rapidly during the early decades of the nineteenth century, and the result was overcrowding, a shortage of water, untreated sewage and disease. To escape these problems, many of the prosperous residents moved their households to impressive villas on the outskirts of the city:

> The villas constructed during this period were distinguished by their large size, their elegance, and their huge gardens. These luxurious houses bore witness to the primary desire for comfort and for a healthy, active, and pleasant family life ...

> Elegance extended to the landscaping of these estates ... More than simply a setting for the beautiful residence, the garden expressed a profound attachment to nature. Thanks to horticulture art, nature was carefully arranged and offered for admiration:

Between 1875 and 1881, a number of large-format, illustrated county, and sometimes provincial, atlases were published in Canada. Included in the volumes were maps of the townships, names of the landowners, plans of towns and villages and engravings of landmark buildings as well as homes. Since the illustrations of the homes were paid for by the proud owners, they present a rather idealized portrait.

The atlases have been reprinted in recent years and continue to provide some details of life in nineteenth-century Canada. This Charlottetown residence shows a typical circular entrance (easier on horse-drawn carriages) and the lively horses and staid cattle so often included in the engravings.

Illustrated Historical Atlas of Prince Edward Island (Belleville: Mika, 1972; facsimile of the 1880 edition)/National Library of Canada 22209

Ravenscrag, the Montreal home of Sir Hugh Allan, one of
the owners of the Montreal Ocean Steamship Company,
photographed in 1902. Many of the large nineteenth-
century houses built by Quebec's successful businessmen
included the kind of elaborate conservatory seen here.

Notman Photographic Archives, McCord Museum of Canadian History,
Montreal/II-143392

flower beds were seeded with flowers and fruit trees, or rare varieties. Paths snaked through a forest, belvederes dominated picturesque sites, and kiosks awaited strollers beside a stream or close to a pond or a fountain. The wealthiest owners built green-houses and hired gardeners from England or Scotland to cultivate plants and exotic fruits.[1]

In this privileged milieu, the delights of nature and artistic expression flourished. Many of the owners of these villas took their gardening very seriously. They joined the recently formed Horticultural Society of Quebec and became intensely interested in the science of horticulture.

Elaborate gardens were established along the Ottawa River in west Quebec. The Montebello gardens were created by Louis-Joseph Papineau, a leader of the Rebellion of 1837 in Lower Canada, and the manoir Saint-Ours has been gardened by the Saint-Ours family for more than two centuries. (The gardens at Montebello are now maintained by Parks Canada.)

For much of the rest of the settled parts of eastern Canada, elegant houses came almost a century later. We see them at their best in the county atlases that were published in the second half of the nineteenth century. The survey material was given without cost

Dr. Dorland's Belleville home, with its much more elaborate structure and grounds, includes unusual weaving pathways and an eye-catching fountain.

Illustrated Historical Atlas of Hastings and Prince Edward Counties (Belleville: Mika, 1972; facsimile of the 1878 edition). National Library of Canada/22210

An extraordinary delphinium garden in the Thunder Bay district, photographed in 1928.

Archives of Ontario/
RG 16-274 (p.52)
AO4824

to publishers, who added some historical and current information, including detailed and romanticized illustrations of some of the buildings in each county. They give us some idea of the landscaping around the homes. Families whose houses were included in the atlases paid for the honour—and, no doubt, an attractive rendition was expected! But these are charming landscapes, with their frisky dogs and lively horses, curving driveways, circular flower beds and nearby orchards.

The second and third generations of newcomers who arrived in Canada after the middle of the nine-

Women in Canmore, Alberta, enjoying a party in the garden in 1918.

teenth century benefited greatly from the work of the farmers and gardeners who had come before them:

> The orchards, the great gardens, and the groves of nut trees planted years ago by the settlers provided lavish fare for the table by the sixties, summer and winter. Hickory, walnuts, and butternuts came from the plantings. Beechnuts from the beechwood could be gathered by the bushel. Apples in half a dozen varieties, two or three kinds of pears, the small sweet sugar plums and the big blue prunes, red, white, and black currants, the strawberry bed and the raspberry patch offered abundant fruit for all the year round.[2]

During the second half of the nineteenth century, southern Ontario was busy clearing the formidable forests, developing agriculture and making provision for roads based on the rigid gridiron surveys that had been completed. The result was that most of the landscape had been completely cleared of the original pine, maple and elm forests. As succeeding generations grew up without the experience of clearing the land and without longing for the trees and landscapes of Europe, attitudes changed and the countryside changed again. New plantings along the imposed gridiron softened the landscape with tree-lined roads, usually of sugar maple with its brilliant fall foliage or American elm and black walnut—all native trees. Some imports continued to be popular, trees such as Norway spruce for its beautiful shape, horse chestnut with its white flowering candles and Lombardy poplars for windbreaks. By now the orange daylily (*Hemerocallis*) and the common lilac (*Syringa vulgaris*) had become suc-

cessful escapees and were so widespread that they were taken for native plants.

In the west, such amenities came later. While more permanent houses and more elaborate gardens were becoming common in eastern Canada, the

This Bow Valley ranch house in Fish Creek, Alberta, shown early in the twentieth century, is surrounded by luxuriant vines and garden.

Glenbow Archives, Calgary, Canada/NA-3812-2

Robert McNeil's home on the prairies is illustrated on the cover of this little book on gardening. The house at the top was his first home, built in 1879. Only five years later, he was living comfortably in the large permanent home shown at the bottom. His book is full of good advice for the settler in the west, including the need for beauty: "We cannot too earnestly recommend the growing of flowers. In the push and hurry of the first years of a settler's life these ornaments of our homes are apt to be neglected; but it will not be found wasted time to give a little attention to these old friends. Their familiar faces smiling on us from day to day will cheer us and make us more contented with the new home and life which opens before us in a new country; while the care of them will provide a recreation after the toils of the day."[3]

National Library of Canada/22215

prairies were just beginning to be homesteaded. Sometimes, however, they were quick to catch up, and the "soddie" was replaced before long with a substantial house. Here, since the climate was less friendly to lush flower and vegetable gardens, the kitchen garden probably grew not much more than potatoes and cabbages so that the homesteader's time and energy could be devoted to the large-scale crops that brought in much-needed cash.

BOUNTIFUL GIFTS OF NATURE

By the mid-nineteenth century, gardeners in the east were finally able to order seeds from nurseries within Canada. In 1827, in what is probably the first formal offering of seeds commercially in Ontario, William W. Custead produced a seed catalogue—"from a desire of placing the bountiful gifts of nature within the reach of his friends and neighbours."[4] The catalogue named twelve agents who took seed orders, offered directions for planting and listed the seeds and plants that were available. These included fruit trees (seventy-nine varieties of apple!), shrubs, greenhouse plants and bulbs. (In *Early Canadian Gardening: An 1827 Nursery Catalogue*, Eileen Woodhead describes each item listed for sale by Custead and the role it played in nineteenth-century gardening.)

In Quebec, it was the Scottish and English settlers who first grew flowers that reminded them of home. In his *Histoire de l'horticulture au Québec*, Gaétan Deschênes noted:

These new inhabitants were familiar with flower gardens and used what they knew from their homeland. As for the francophones of the 18th and 19th centuries, all their energy was devoted to building their homes and feeding their families.[5]

In 1860 Auguste Dupuis established the first commercial nursery in Quebec. From a small village on the south shore of the St. Lawrence, he offered a wide range of plants and seeds and provided much-needed advice on the best methods of caring for them. His early catalogues were in the language of his first clients, the wealthy English of Montreal who bought plants and trees for their summer homes along the St. Lawrence. Before long, Dupuis was publishing a French catalogue as well. He was an important figure in the development of gardening in French Canada and a respected expert on the cultivation of fruit trees:

Many Quebeckers profited from his generosity, his advice and his initiatives. His life was a lesson in energy, honesty, and work, and a good example from which the many young people who came in contact with him were able to benefit.[6]

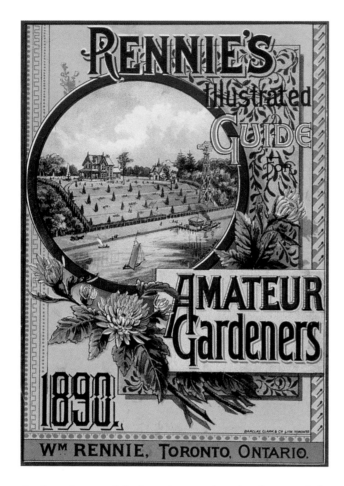

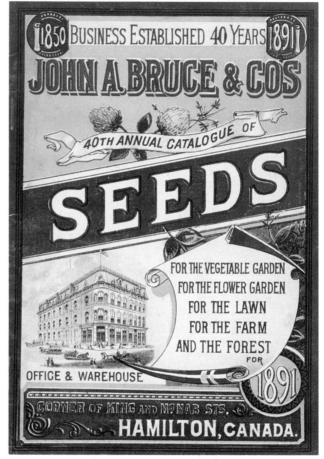

Seed catalogues of the late nineteenth and early twentieth centuries allowed artists the freedom to create glowing covers and perfect line drawings of flowers and vegetables inside, as the examples on these three pages illustrate. Spring dreams of gardeners have changed very little over the past century!

Centre for Canadian Historical Horticultural Studies, Royal Botanical Gardens, Hamilton, Ontario

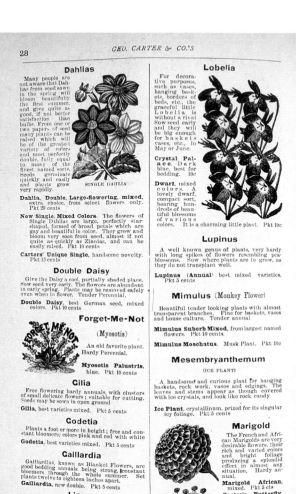

Centre for Canadian Historical Horticultural Studies, Royal Botanical Gardens, Hamilton, Ontario

These catalogues, and the others that followed soon after, were at first just lists of the available plants and seeds, along with their prices. It wasn't long, however, before the nurseries were outdoing each other with beautiful illustrations and colour printing, first on the covers, later on the inside pages. These early catalogues, with their paintings and drawings of flowers, vegetables and landscapes, have a delicate, idealistic quality that has been lost in today's harsher photographic renditions.

REFRESHMENT FOR BODY AND MIND

Public parks, designed solely for people to enjoy, did not become a part of city life until the middle of the nineteenth century. Early Canadian towns and villages usually had a green space of some kind—commons where cattle or other livestock grazed and often public squares where people met for civic occasions or where market days were held. Port-Royal, Saint John, Quebec, Montreal and Toronto all had public or market squares from their days as early settlements. J.R. Wright in *Urban Parks in Ontario* tells of a unique public lot enjoyed by the citizens of St. John's, Newfoundland, as early as 1583. Although it was just an empty lot where wildflowers and berries grew, it was called "The Garden" and was a favourite place for

The Halifax Public Gardens have been one of the most popular spots in the city for nearly 130 years. The central, ornamental bandstand, erected in 1887 in honour of Queen Victoria's Jubilee, is surrounded by flowers, many of them laid out in the carpet bedding style popular in the middle of the nineteenth century.

Nova Scotia Museum of Natural History/B00994/Photograph by A. Wilson

65

Many of the most productive and attractive gardens from as early as the seventeenth century flourished behind the walls of the religious institutions of New France. In 1657 Marguerite de Bourgeoys established the Congrégation de Notre Dame in Montreal and there opened her first school for girls. This picture, taken about 1885, illustrates the beauty and serenity of the congregation's community garden.

Notman Photograph Archives, McCord Museum of Canadian History, Montreal/MP-0000.2924/Photograph by Oliver B. Buell

the citizens to walk and enjoy nature. It might even be considered a forerunner to our present-day city parks. In some cities, cemeteries were used for picnics and recreation in the first half of the century. But the idea of creating a treed and grassy area for pleasure and recreation, financed by the local government and accessible to all, only began to catch on in the middle of the nineteenth century.

The earliest recorded city park was Victoria Park, created in 1842 in the east end of London, England. It was popular from the outset, and before the end of the decade, almost every town in England had its own park. The idea spread quickly from England to Upper Canada (Ontario). By the 1850s there were public parks in Kingston, Toronto, Hamilton and Niagara-on-the-Lake.

THE WRITING GARDENERS

Advice on gardening in the Canadian climate was in very short supply for most of the nineteenth century, but here and there material began to appear. By the end of the century, there were articles and newspaper columns offering gardening tips, and even a few books.

Catharine Parr Traill was one of the first to publish specific gardening information and advice. In *The Backwoods of Canada*, published in 1836, she wrote of her life as an immigrant pioneer and included some of her early gardening experiences. Later she wrote about her gardens in more detail in *The Canadian Settler's Guide*, published in 1855:

> Rhubarbs should always find a place in your garden; a cool, shady place and rich soil is best: throw on the bed in the Fall a good supply of long dung, and dig it in in the Spring. A barrel without a bottom put over a good plant, or a frame of an old box, will make the stalks very tender and less acid. The Giant Rhubarb is the best kind to plant.
>
> A bed of Carraways should also find a place in your garden; it is always useful, and the seeds sell well, besides being valuable as a cattle medicine.
>
> A good bed of pot-herbs is essential. I would bring out seeds of Balm, Thyme, and Sweet Basil, for these are rarely met with here. –Sage, Savory, Mint and Peppermint, are easily got.
>
> Sweet Marjoram is not commonly met with. I would also bring out some nice flower-seeds, and also vegetable seeds of good kinds, especially fine sorts of cabbage. You should learn to save your seeds. Good seeds will meet with a market at the stores.[7]

Traill also included short articles on pumpkins, squash, cucumbers, melons and beans, as well as other vegetables and fruit of all kinds, including tomatoes, which had been considered poisonous earlier in the century, but were being cultivated by the 1850s.

She considered hops to be the most useful plant in a settler's garden.

James Dougall, a Scottish immigrant, played an important role in the history of southwestern Ontario. He operated the family dry goods business in Windsor and was active politically, first as an alderman and then as mayor of the city he is said to have named. He had a lifelong interest in horticulture, and his home, Rosebank, was renowned for its gardens and crops. In 1850 he established Windsor Nurseries. He wrote frequently on gardening, and in 1867 he published a small book entitled *The Canadian Fruit-culturist; or, Letters to an Intending Fruit-grower*. It was the first original book published in English Canada on the growing of fruit.

It was five years later before the first complete book on gardening in Canada was published. The *Canadian Fruit, Flower, and Kitchen Gardener*, written by D.W. Beadle, appeared in 1872. It covered the field thoroughly. Beadle had spent eighteen years as a nurseryman in the family business in St. Catharines. In 1859 he had been one of the founders of the Fruit Growers' Association of Upper Canada; he remained an active member of the organization and served as its secretary for many years. Beadle wrote articles on gardening for *Canadian Farmer*, and in 1878 he became the editor of *Canadian Horticulturist*, the monthly magazine of the Fruit Growers' Association

the ovary it penetrates it, and coming in contact with the germs that are in the ovary, fertilizes them, or in other words, imparts

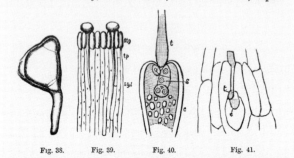

Fig. 38.   Fig. 39.   Fig. 40.   Fig. 41.

to them the power of growth and development into perfect seeds. In Fig. 40, *t* represents the lower end of this pollen rootlet entering the ovary, and in Fig. 41 it is seen after it has entered the ovary and come in contact with the germ *e*. Fig. 42 represents an apple blossom cut in two, and by comparing this with Fig. 37, it will be seen that the apple blossom has three pistils, while the cherry blossom has but one. This diversity exists in a yet greater degree in the strawberry blossom, which has a very great number of pistils; but whatever the number of pistils, the process is ever the same, the pollen must reach the germ through the pistil or pistils, or the germ will perish, and in the case of numerous pistils, it will be seen that each pistil supplies its own division of the seed vessel or ovary with the needed pollen. That these organs may be the more readily recognized, they are shown separate from the flower. Figure 43 shows, at the left hand, the stamen, with the anther on the top, from which

Fig. 42.

In his chapter "The Production of New Varieties," Beadle carefully explains what is known about "this most fascinating field of study and experiment, one that has as yet been but very partially explored, and that offers to the Canadian fruit grower the opportunity of producing varieties of fruit adapted to our own peculiar climate that shall far surpass the majority of those now in cultivation." On this page Beadle illustrates how the ovary, pistil, stamen and pollen of a blossom create a new seed.

D.W. Beadle, *Canadian Fruit, Flower, and Kitchen Gardener* (Toronto: James Campbell, 1872), 57/National Library of Canada/22211

of Ontario. In his first issue Beadle wrote: "The lover of fruits is also usually a lover of flowers, and delights to surround the house with a well kept lawn ..." With this in mind, he made certain that the magazine was of interest to gardeners and growers of all kinds of plants, trees and bushes.

Fruit growing was so important to early Canadians that it is not surprising to see that almost half of the 390 pages in Beadle's *Canadian Fruit, Flower, and Kitchen Gardener* are devoted to the "Fruit Garden." Propagation and pruning, transplanting and mulching, and protection from insects and mice are all covered. Beadle describes sixteen different kinds of fruit-bearing trees and plants in detail, from the apple (thirty-five varieties) to the huckleberry (which he called a "neglected fruit"). The rest of the book is devoted to the kitchen garden, the flower garden and the growing of ever-greens. "The Kitchen Garden deserves more attention from our farmers than it has generally received," he wrote.

> The products of a good garden are worth all that they cost, for the single purpose of supplying the farmer's table with that variety of food which the best development of body and mind require. It is no uncommon thing to find the table of a well-to-do farmer very scantily supplied with vegetables. Beyond that great staple, the potato, there is seldom any vegetable on the table, year in and year out ... This is a great mistake ... A well-stocked and well-kept garden is a sure concomitant of a more intelligent and more refined yeomanry.[8]

It would be many years before this excellent gardening guide was supplanted.

The best known of the early garden columnists of the period was Annie L. Jack. One of those energetic nineteenth-century women, she managed to raise eleven children with her husband, Robert Jack, at Châteauguay in Lower Canada (Quebec) while growing enough vegetables to feed the family and to sell. Her garden started as a small plot on the family farm but expanded as she planted trees, shrubs and vines around the homestead. At the same time she was writing frequently about the work involved. Eventually the

Gardeners' tools have not changed very much over the century, as can be seen in this page from the 1910 catalogue of Dupuy & Ferguson.

Centre for Canadian Historical Horticultural Studies, Royal Botanical Gardens, Hamilton, Ontario

The invention of the home lawnmower in 1830 significantly changed the look of Canadian homes and gardens. By the second half of the century, the rough, scythed sward around many homes became a closely mown, spacious lawn. *The Elms*, this charming wash drawing by Reverend William Arthur Johnson, shows an elegantly dressed woman in 1879 pushing what must have been one of the earliest mowers in the country.

Toronto Reference Library/MTL 1312

Jacks were selling shrubs, fruit trees, and plants from the farm and shipping apples to England. On top of all this gardening activity, Jack was writing poems and short stories, which were published widely in the United States, and she was active as a member and contributor to the Montreal Horticultural Society and the Fruit Growers' Association of the Province of Quebec. Her column in the *Montreal Daily Witness*, called "Garden Talks," had a strong moral tone and ran from 1898 to 1903. In her column Jack described her personal gardening experiences and answered questions from readers. In 1903 the column led to a small book, *The Canadian Garden: A Pocket Help for the Amateur.* Along with concise, helpful advice for the new gardener, she included a monthly calendar of "reminders"—a favourite organizational tool for garden writers. Her June reminders end with this comment: "Just now the watchword is—Keep hoeing!" She calls December "the resting month of the year."

The Canadian Garden Book, published fifteen years later, was the second book of gardening advice written by a Canadian woman, Adele H. Austen. Austen had a very different life than Annie Jack. Daughter of a wealthy Toronto family, she worked and managed the garden at the famous family home called Spadina.

> In my own garden the space allotted to "eats" is about 50 x 50 feet, just a corner of the whole—which is only half an acre—but what it does produce! Intensive farming intensified! ...we were able to feed a family of four adults, often sitting down to a dinner with seven home-grown vegetables, besides canning many quarts of beets and tomatoes.[9]

Austen wrote under the pseudonym Dorothy Perkins, the name of a popular rose of the day. She was clearly an anglophile when it came to gardening: "As a nation we are just learning the spirit of Gardening—

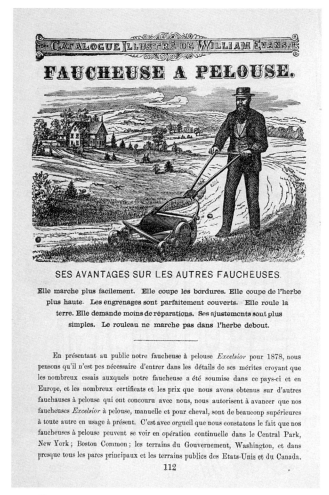

A William Evans catalogue from 1878 shows one of the early lawnmowers available in Canada.

Centre for Canadian Historical Horticultural Studies, Royal Botanical Gardens, Hamilton, Ontario

A horticultural
class working in the
vegetable gardens at the Macdonald Institute's Women's
College of Domestic Arts in Guelph.

Archives of Ontario ACC 2313/S4347

Women from the horticultural class
during the 1915 winter term.

Archives of Ontario ACC 2313/S4346

as they have it in England."[10] However, Austen advised
Canadians to leave formal gardens to the continent
and to create instead "homey" gardens. Above all,
she admonished her readers: "Relax! Most of you live
in a whirl. Your threadbare, overstrained nerves are
crying out for relaxation. Help create a Canadian garden picture!"[11]

PLANNING THE LANDSCAPE

The idea that the land around public buildings
required attention and planning by someone with special training came late to Canada. One of the earliest
landscape gardeners, or landscape architects as they
became know, was Henry A. Engelhardt. He arrived in
Canada in 1870 from Prussia via the United States,
where he had worked with Frederick Olmsted on the
design for Central Park in New York City. He immediately won commissions to beautify the grounds of
the Ontario Institute for the Education of the Blind in
Brantford and the Ontario Institute for the Deaf and
Dumb (now Sir James Whitney School for the Deaf) in
Belleville. But he is best known for his work designing Ontario cemeteries. These included the civic
cemeteries in Port Hope and Belleville and, most
notably, the extensive rolling grounds of Mount
Pleasant Cemetery in Toronto. Laid out with shade
trees, winding walks and colourful flower beds,

Today, Mount Pleasant Cemetery lives up to its name as a
green and leafy park where Torontonians can still enjoy
the beautiful landscape created by Henry A. Engelhardt in
the nineteenth century.

Photograph by Jeremy Martin

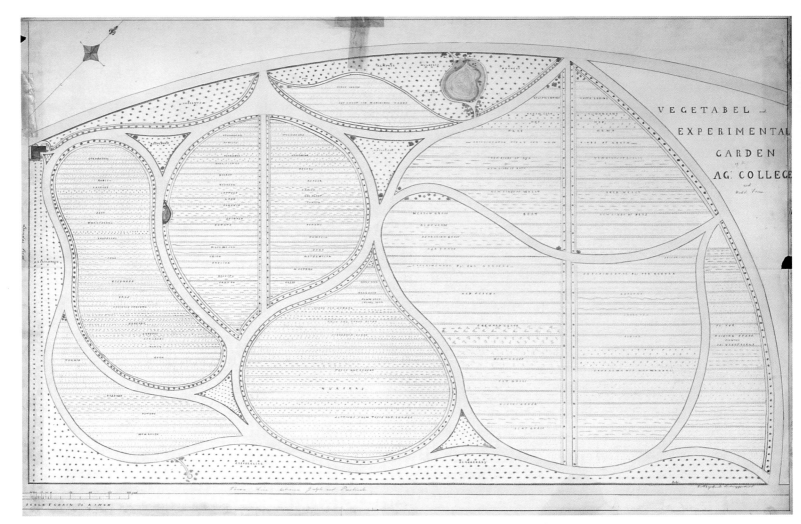

Henry A. Engelhardt created three landscape plans for the
Ontario Agricultural College in 1874. Among them is this
lovely curving garden design (detail on facing page).

Archives of Ontario RG 16-41

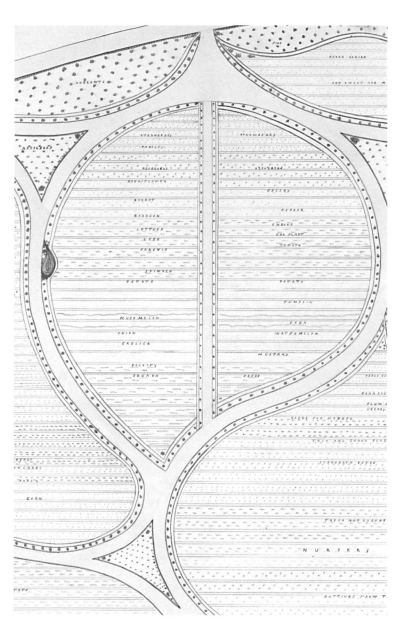

Mount Pleasant soon became a favourite place for family outings and picnics. Before long the city extended the streetcar line and set its timetable so that Torontonians could enjoy holiday trips to the cemetery. (Brantford and Calgary were among the other cities that extended their streetcar lines for the same purpose.)

Engelhardt had strong opinions on cemeteries and their design. He believed that each city should have only one cemetery and it should not be situated on church grounds:

> The site for a cemetery should be well chosen, at some distance from the turmoil and bustle of active life. Yet should be always easy of access. If the site chosen possesses natural advantages, such as hills and dales, groves and creeks, so much the better, but the improvements should agree and conform to the natural features of the place.[12] 🖘

5
Reforming the Landscape

PASSION FOR REFORM

A passion for reform, referred to as the social gospel, swept through most of the western world in the last decade of the nineteenth century. With it came pressure for everything from fair wages for workers to improving the natural environment of the cities. Considered "one of the most significant single features in the complexion of social reform in Canada,"[1] the social gospel influenced thinking in almost every area of Canadian life.

The social gospel was driven by the evangelical Christian movement but was not strictly religious. This new sense of social justice and personal morality was developing just at a time when there was general agreement that urban life must be improved. Much of its impetus came from the deplorable state of many Canadian cities. Industrialization had brought slums, overcrowding and unhealthy living conditions.

The desire to improve people's lives encouraged a new interest in the landscape and a growing belief in the restorative power of flowers, trees and gardens. Edwinna von Baeyer, garden and landscape historian, has written of the influence the reform movement had on gardening in Canada in her valuable book on this period, *Rhetoric and Roses: A History of Canadian Gardening 1900-1930.* "Never has the craft of gardening had to bear such heavy psychological, social and moral burdens," she writes. "Beauty ceased to be the main goal; it now struggled for a place alongside good citizenship, improvement, social remedy, morality and material progress."[2]

The horticultural changes aimed at improving the lives of ordinary people would eventually transform Canada's landscape. Parks were created in many

The CPR station garden at Moose Jaw, Saskatchewan, in September 1906.

Industrialization in the nineteenth century created city slums like this one, photographed in downtown Quebec City about 1890. Partly in response to conditions such as these, the City Beautiful Movement was born, bringing with it recreation grounds and city parks.

Notman Photographic Archives, McCord Museum of Canadian History, Montreal/view-2335

Although the Canadian population had remained fairly static during the final decades of the nineteenth century, the early years of the twentieth century saw a significant increase in immigration. This, along with a high birth rate and decreasing death rate, meant that the population was growing very quickly. At the same time, what had once been very much an agricultural economy was moving to an industrial one. At the end of the nineteenth century, only about a third of the population was living in cities; twenty years later, this had increased to 50 per cent. The cities could not expand quickly enough to accommodate the increase comfortably. The result, in many cities, was ugly slums.

cities so that workers could enjoy the natural world and escape the harsh realities of urban life for a time. Gardening was introduced into the school curriculum in many provinces as educators sought ways to contribute to the moral improvement of their students. And the beautification of public spaces, known as the City Beautiful Movement, was undertaken for the pleasure of city dwellers (and ultimately for the benefit of business). Even the railways got into the act.

NATURE IN THE CITIES

Although the first city parks appeared around the middle of the nineteenth century, a city parks movement didn't really get underway until three or four decades later. "Indeed, the years between 1883 and 1914 saw not only the general acceptance of the need for public recreational grounds, but also development of parks at a scale unequalled in relative terms in Canada until the post-World War II Years."[3]

Frederick Law Olmsted, an American landscape architect full of new and creative ideas, exerted a major influence on park design throughout North America during the second half of the nineteenth century. In Canada he was involved directly in only a few specific projects, but his legacy can still be seen in the style of many of the parks found in our cities today.

Along with his partner, Olmsted had been responsible for the design of New York's Central Park in 1858. Drawing heavily on the English landscape tradition, he saw parks as natural landscapes—but natural landscapes improved by design. His principles for park design included areas where roads for vehicles would be separated from the graceful curving walkways for people. Buildings would be kept to a minimum, and flowers would bloom in natural-shaped beds of single species, sometimes clustered around buildings. Light

The Woolverton family played a significant role in the history of horticulture in Canada. They originally settled in the Niagara peninsula in 1802. Linus, born in 1846, was a respected fruit grower with two books to his credit. He succeeded D.W. Beadle as secretary of the Fruit Growers' Association of Ontario and later as editor of *Canadian Horticulturist*. He was greatly interested in encouraging the improvement of home landscapes and was active in the City Beautiful Movement. His son, C. Ernest Woolverton, studied horticulture at the Ontario Agricultural College (now part of the University of Guelph) and went on to become Canada's first native-born landscape architect. He was responsible for the design of two parks in Sarnia as well as a number of residential projects.

Mount Royal, a magnificent park in the heart of Montreal.

Photograph by Malak, Ottawa

and airy bandstands and pergolas would be important elements in a well-designed park, as would homogeneous wooded areas and meadows linking spaces set aside for recreation. Olmsted also favoured beautiful vistas of water and distant horizons.

In 1877 Olmsted was hired to design Mount Royal Park in Montreal. The idea of creating a public park on Mount Royal had been discussed on and off

from as early as 1850, but more than twenty years went by before steps were taken to purchase land for the site. Originally, the site was considered to be too far from the city to benefit most people (today it is situated in the heart of the city), but in spite of this and other difficulties, Olmsted moved ahead with the design. Mount Royal Park became—and remains— one of Montreal's major landmarks.

During the later years of the nineteenth century, things progressed rapidly: parks were created in cities all across the country, landscape architecture became a recognized profession, agricultural colleges sprang up to train farmers and horticulturists, and governments created departments to oversee the development and maintenance of public parks. In Ontario the Public Parks Act was passed in 1883, and in 1897 the Act to Encourage the Planting and Growing of Trees recommended plantings on streets, lanes, squares and highways. Much of this work fell to horticultural societies and garden clubs, many of which were just getting established about this time.

In Manitoba, which had entered Confederation in 1870, the growing of trees was the main focus of horticultural activity. This was still a period of early settlement, and trees in the province's open landscape not only were a comfort to the settlers but also provided windbreaks to protect their farms. Within the micro-climates created by these tree plantings, gardens began to flourish. By 1883 the province's 9077 farmers were devoting 1400 hectares of their land to orchards and gardens. In 1886 Manitoba instituted Arbour Day, following the lead of the Northwest Territories (including what later became Saskatchewan and Alberta), which had declared an annual tree-planting day in 1884.

In 1892 Manitoba passed its own parks bill, modelled on that of Ontario. Social reformers and business interests co-operated, sometimes with more passion than logic, to press for more green space

Public parks usually included bandshells, pavilions and elaborate fountains, such as those seen here at Allan Gardens, Toronto, in about 1890. Both the pavilion and the fountain were destroyed by fire in 1902.

Archives of Ontario/ACC 2728 st 108

within the cities. In an 1898 editorial, the Winnipeg magazine *Town Topics* argued:

> unless parks were established and speedily, half the inhabitants would quickly die of asphyxiation of want of "breathing spaces", capital would forsake the town on account of its forbidding aspect, and the babies, heaven bless them, would perish miserably for lack of room in which to exercise their chubby limbs and expand their developing lungs.[4]

By 1900 urban beautification was the policy in Winnipeg, the first major city on the prairies. Trees were planted along the streets and on the boulevards. A network of parks was established: twenty-seven

One of the floral displays on Parliament Hill in Ottawa, about 1900.

civic and three private parks were created in the city between 1893 and 1914.[5]

Frederick G. Todd was a landscape architect and one of Olmsted's protégés. He had come from the United States to Montreal, where he was involved with Olmsted's work on Mount Royal Park. Later he was responsible for a number of important park developments from St. John's to Vancouver. He developed

A view of Queen Victoria Park, Niagara Falls. Almost every Canadian city had a park named Victoria at the end of the nineteenth century. Influenced by Olmsted, the Ontario government had passed an act to protect the Niagara Falls area, and in 1888 the sixty-hectare Queen Victoria Park was opened to the public. Since then the Niagara Parks Commission has expanded it to almost 1200 hectares of beautiful parkland between Niagara-on-the-Lake and Port Erie. On its grounds is the Niagara Falls Botanical Gardens School of Horticulture, the only residential school of its kind in Canada.

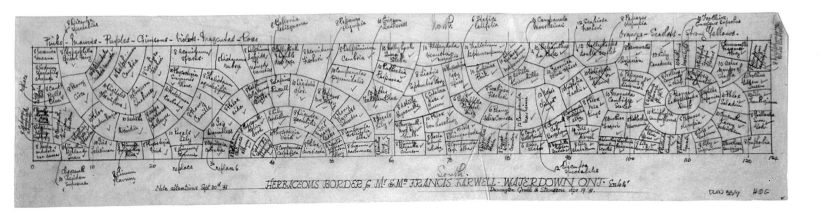

plans for the national capital in Ottawa (which were never implemented), for Battlefields Park in Quebec City and for Assiniboine Park in Winnipeg. With the creation of Saskatchewan in 1905, Todd was commissioned to develop a plan for the provincial legislature's sixty-eight–hectare site. The result was Wascana Park, where more than 100,000 trees and shrubs, from nurseries throughout North America and Europe, were planted. A few years later, under the renowned British landscape architect Thomas Mawson, an elaborate pattern of formal hedges and flower beds was laid out around the legislative buildings—a demonstration of what could be accomplished on the arid Palliser Triangle with sufficient will and adequate investment.

Lorrie and Howard Dunington-Grubb arrived in Canada in 1911, both having already enjoyed careers as

The firm of Dunington-Grubb did a wide range of landscaping work, from garden plans for private homes to larger government projects. This pencil sketch of the plan for an herbaceous border at the Farwell home in Waterdown, Ontario, was prepared in 1941.

Dunington-Grubb & Stensson Collection, Archival and Special Collections, University of Guelph Library

landscape architects in England. Howard Dunington-Grubb described the gardening situation as it seemed to them when they opened an office in Toronto:

> In the boom year of 1911 Canadians were so preoccupied with unearned increment that gardening imagination reached no further than a few beds of geraniums planted by the local florist. An attempt was made to keep the wolf from the door by trying to show real estate speculators that the gridiron was not the only method of laying out streets.[6]

TORONTO CITY PLANNING BOARD
UNIVERSITY AVENUE
DUNINGTON-GRUBB & STENSSON
Landscape Architects

The plan for University Avenue in Toronto was developed by Dunington-Grubb & Stensson between 1961 and 1965. Howard Dunington-Grubb did the overall design. Janina Stensson designed two of the islands and her husband, Howard Stensson, contributed the triangular planters.

Dunington-Grubb & Stensson Collection, Archival and Special Collections, University of Guelph Library

In spite of slow going in the early days, the Dunington-Grubbs were eventually successful in establishing themselves as landscape architects and were exceedingly active in the field. Both were founding members of the Canadian Society of Landscape Architects and worked on many projects, ranging from Toronto subdivisions to the Rainbow Bridge Gardens at Niagara Falls, as well as a large number of private residences. In 1913 they founded Sheridan Nurseries to supply ornamental trees and shrubs that were not then readily available in Canada. The following year, they hired Sven Herman Stensson and his family from England to manage the nursery business.

All this extraordinary activity benefited from the work of a number of different groups, in addition to the social reformers. These included educators and child advocates looking to provide recreation and natural environments for children, civic officials and politicians interested in luring business to their area, developers hoping to improve profits, and companies trying to attract and satisfy workers. Uncoordinated though these efforts were, they resulted in the development of civic parks across the country. War and the Depression cut back on park development for some decades, but relief programs and centennial celebrations would contribute to their construction in the future.

THE MACDONALD MOVEMENT

James Wilson Robertson, an early education expert and reformer working around the turn of the twentieth century, believed that the lives of rural people would be greatly improved if practical information about current farming and gardening methods was more widely available. By giving young people the information and knowledge they needed to be successful farmers, Robertson hoped that they would be more inclined to stay on the farm. His view was shared by Sir William Macdonald, a Montreal tobacco merchant and philanthropist. Education was a passion for Macdonald. He gave endowments to Macdonald College in Quebec and Macdonald Hall in Ontario and generous bequests to McGill University and the Ontario Agricultural College. Together these two men devised a campaign that became known as the Macdonald Movement for the Improvement of Rural Conditions, or simply as the Macdonald Movement.

Gardening in the schools was one of the most successful elements of the movement. It began as an experiment with twenty-five schools in Nova Scotia, New Brunswick, Prince Edward Island, Quebec and Ontario. Teachers received special training to help them supervise their students' horticultural projects. School gardens were planted and tended by the children, and they were encouraged to start a garden at home as well. The movement broadened into what were known as Consolidated Schools, financed by Macdonald. "Each pupil had his or her own garden and, as well, the girls shared a kitchen garden and the boys experimental farm crop plots."[7]

The results were impressive. Not only were the young gardeners more likely to remain in school, but students in the program in Ontario (where figures are available) achieved higher marks overall on the standard provincial high school entrance exams:

> In 1906, in Carleton County, in schools without gardens 49 per cent of the candidates passed, while those who came from the five schools to which were attached gardens 71 per cent were successful. Apparently the work with the hands in the garden increased the capacity for work with books.[8]

The Ontario Department of Education underlined the benefits in 1912 in a publication designed to encourage students in their gardening and record keeping: "Keeping a Garden journal will help you to become a good gardener as well as a good scholar."[9]

The idea of including gardening in the curriculum spread across the west. In Alberta, with its rural population, the program was particularly popular, although perhaps not always completely successful:

> Early annual reports abound in pictures of such activities showing sad-faced little boys and girls

Poplar Point School, Manitoba, about 1910. In 1913 the federal government's Agricultural Instruction Act allotted grants to the provinces to encourage activities such as school gardens. By 1915 there were more than 400 school gardens in Manitoba.

Public Archives of Manitoba/W.J. Sisler Collection 77/N11610

hoeing and raking and weeding their vegetable and flower plots under the grim supervision of their teachers. Time after time the inspectors report on the growing success of the school garden programme, although not all comments are laudatory, as for example this from Inspector M.E. Lazerte: "There are too many cases where the little mound of earth serves to mark the grave of the seed or of the early-departed plant."[10]

The Macdonald Movement was part of a more general alliance of various groups extolling the virtues of country life and a moral life in general. Known as the Country Life Movement, the alliance supported school gardens among many other reforms. School gardens survived sporadically, particularly during times of war. But the Consolidated Schools, although supported to an extent by Macdonald, Robertson and provincial governments, proved to be more expensive than local ratepayers were willing to maintain (in spite of the fact that because students stayed in school longer, the cost per student was often lower). Gradually, the Macdonald Movement ceased to play the major role it had during the early decades of the century.

BEAUTY BY RAIL

The last spike completing the Canadian Pacific Railway was driven in November 1885, and the line was carrying passengers across the west by the following summer. As it acquired land along the way, the CPR became involved in encouraging settlement on the prairies. Increased traffic was needed to ensure that the line was successful. What better way to convince possible settlers of the fertility of the land than by encouraging displays of flowers, shrubs and trees at the stations? This idea coincided nicely with the new interest in beautifying public spaces. It also responded to the landscaping interests of many people employed at the stations. Some were already familiar with station gardens back home in Europe and wanted to make improvements to the ugly landscape left behind from construction of the CPR line.

Two men in particular are credited with getting the station gardens underway. N. Stewart Dunlop, who worked for the CPR in Montreal, began in a small way in the 1890s by sending out a few packets of seeds to employees who had expressed an interest in planting flowers around their stations. At the same time, David Hysop, an immigrant homesteader in Manitoba who also worked for the CPR, was suggesting that gardens at the stations would be a good way to promote the land. The idea caught on quickly with station agents all along the line.

The early station gardeners grew mostly annuals—hollyhocks, nasturtiums, sweet peas, geraniums, alyssum, petunias, stocks, larkspur, phlox, cannas, salvia, asters and morning glories. Soon spring bulbs and perennial beds were added, with bleeding hearts, campanula, peonies and roses.

By 1908 the CPR had set up its own forestry department. The department established nurseries to supply shrubs and perennials to CPR employees interested in creating permanent plantings around their stations. Four years later, a horticulturist, Dr. Gustaf A. Bosson-Krook, was hired in Wolseley, Saskatchewan, to give direction and advice to the gardeners. A picture from 1917 shows a nursery field of 70,000 three-year-old caragana shrubs!

From as early as 1916, the *Canadian Pacific Railway Bulletin* was including pictures of attractively laid-out station gardens from British Columbia to New Brunswick. (In the east, improving the station landscapes became part of the City Beautiful Movement.) Formal gardens were favoured, with round centre beds and geometric paths, often with "CPR" or the station's name spelled out in whitewashed stones or colourful flowers. The gardens ranged from only a few beds right around the station to impressive landscapes spread over several hectares. The section houses and bunkhouse were often surrounded by flowers, which were cared for by the workers. At first the gardens were labours of love on the part of station agents; later on, particularly in the larger centres, experienced gardeners were hired.

As time went by, the CPR's forestry department took more and more control over these activities. Department officials travelled to inspect proposed garden sites and started designing garden plans. Before long, there began to be a recognizable railway garden look. In 1923 the forestry department moved to Winnipeg, and six years later Manitoba's provincial horticulturist, J.R. Almey, was hired to head it. Almey served the station gardens for thirty-one years. During those years, greenhouses were established in eight centres: Fort William, Kenora, Winnipeg, Moose Jaw, Ogden, Revelstoke, Kamloops and Vancouver. By the 1940s the department was regularly shipping to 1250 employees across the country some 10,000 packets of annual seeds—an automatic selection of alyssum, cornflower, clarkia, scarlet flax, Shirley poppy, California poppy, nasturtium and zinnia. For the more serious station gardeners—up to 200 of them—an additional seventy species were available.

The forestry department gradually acquired more knowledge of the differing horticultural requirements in all the widely varied regions the railway line passed through. It not only supplied the stations with seeds, bedding plants, perennials, shrubs, trees (for decoration and windbreaks) and fertilizer, but also awarded about $1000 in yearly prizes. Although station gardens were eligible from all seven provinces traversed by the CPR, it was in the difficult prairie climate that most of the CPR's award-winning gardens were found. Here the station gardeners had succeeded in establishing flourishing gardens in the dry conditions that often prevailed there, in spite of having to carry water by hand since no "laid on" water was available.

As times and fashions changed, some of the formal garden beds around the stations gave way to more natural plantings. "In Alberta, for example, station gardens at Fort Macleod and Red Deer were designed to be natural and parklike."[11]

Other railway lines such as the Grand Trunk and, in particular, the Canadian National began similar garden programs, and eventually Canadian railway gardens became famous both inside and outside the country. Sadly, this touch of beauty slowly disappeared. After the Second World War the railways cut their garden program budgets, and as time went by, the increasing use of automobiles and other means of transportation meant that rail travel itself was declining. More and more, land around the stations was paved over for the convenience of car-driving customers. Now we can only look enviously at the

intriguing pictures from earlier days and admire what was accomplished.

In the 1930s the social gospel movement began to fade as a force for social change. As a more complex society developed, however, many of its objectives were absorbed by government departments, unions, political parties and other organizations. The gardening and public landscaping ideas that had been fostered by the movement and that seemed so new at the turn of the century became an accepted part of community planning a few decades later. Something about the pictures and words that have come down to us

One of the most elaborate gardens along the railway was at Kenora, Ontario. It looks here as though its well-kept paths might be accessible to travellers, something that was true of few of the station gardens.

Canadian Pacific Archives/NS-13001

from this period remains uniquely touching. We might be amused, even embarrassed, at the idea of gardening as "an ennobling influence,"[12] but it is still possible to empathize with the feelings that inspired that idea. ❧

PROCEEDINGS

CONNECTED WITH THE FORMATION

OF

THE MONTREAL

HORTICULTURAL SOCIETY,

AND ITS

CONSTITUTION.

MONTREAL,

PRINTED BY J. STARKE & COMPANY.

1847.

6
Talking About Gardening

Sharing gardening information and talking about successes and failures must be one of the most enjoyable experiences for a gardener. Even today, when so much (perhaps too much!) information is readily available in libraries and bookstores, on radio and television and now on the Internet, personal discussion remains more satisfying. Imagine then how important it must have been in earlier times, when seeds were hard to come by and little information was available about what could survive and what would flourish in the Canadian climate.

We will probably never know when the first garden club or horticultural society met. Neighbours undoubtedly traded information and seeds from the days of the first settlers. Catharine Parr Traill certainly advocated it. Later many organized but informal meetings would have gone unrecorded, and of the many early records that were kept only a few have survived. We know that there were garden clubs and horticultural societies meeting from east to west before the turn of the twentieth century. Over the years, they all traded seeds and information, held flower shows, beautified public spaces, raised food in time of war and worked together to develop special gardens for the benefit of others. In many cases it was the members of the garden clubs and horticultural societies who researched and recorded the history of gardening in the various regions of Canada. In 1967, during the country's centennial year, a number of local gardening histories were published by these groups.

The formality of this early document recording the founding of one of the first horticultural associations reveals how serious members were about their activities.

GETTING ORGANIZED

The first formal organization of gardeners seems to have been in Montreal, and there are a number of different dates for its various incarnations. The Montreal Florist Society met first in February of 1811 and held a show that same year. In 1817 the organization was renamed the Society of Horticulture of Montreal.[1] The *Encyclopedia of Gardening,* published in England in 1850, records that a *"horticultural society* was established in Montreal about 1830, and though after a few years it was comparatively neglected, in 1834 it was revived."[2] Writing in 1831, Joseph Bouchette mentions that there were associations in both Quebec and Montreal, "which have led to considerable ameliorations in the culture of garden fruits and vegetables."[3] The National Library of Canada has a document from 1847 that records the formation of a horticultural society that year: "Upon this ground, then, of its tendency to improve our moral and intellectual nature would I persuade our fellow-citizens to aid us in our endeavour to establish and maintain the Society ..."[4] How formal it sounds, almost as though written for the history books. This group clearly took themselves seriously. By 1858 the editor of the *Canadian Horticulturist* was able to write that there was then a flourishing horticultural society, and "probably more glass structures for fruits and flowers

TORONTO

HORTICULTURAL SOCIETY.

PATRON:
His Excellency the Governor General.

OFFICE BEARERS FOR 1861.

President:
THE HON. G. W. ALLAN.

First Vice-President—SHERIFF JARVIS.
Second Vice-President—F. W. COATE, Esq.

Secretaries:
J. C. SMALL. | J. GILBERT.

Treasurer:
J. C. SMALL.

Directors:

PROFESSOR CROFT,	HON. W. CAYLEY,
PROFESSOR HINCKS,	HOMER DIXON,
STEPHEN HEWARD,	H. MILLER,
JOHN GRAY,	J. FLEMING,
J. D. HUMPHREYS,	J. E. PELL.
J. G. BEARD,	J. A. SIMMERS,
RICE LEWIS,	S. ASHBY,
G. LESLIE,	J. BEACHELL.
JNO. RITCHEY, Jr.,	

National Library of Canada/22213

in Montreal than in any other city of the same population on our continent."[5]

In 1863 explorer and naturalist Henry Youle Hind noted that there were horticultural societies in Toronto (founded in 1834), Hamilton, Kingston, Peterborough, St. Catharines, Niagara, Cobourg and Paris. He was particularly impressed by the growth of interest in gardening that had taken place in Toronto over the previous twenty years. Although only two small greenhouses could be found in the city in 1836, he wrote:

> In 1862, there exist many thousand feet of glass-roofed structures, most of them built upon the most approved modern principles, and adapted to the growth of foreign grapes, green-house and exotic plants. Orchard houses are already numerous, and a taste for the delightful pursuit of horticulture is rapidly spreading.[6]

In the early days, with a small population and the difficulties involved in organizing the various segments of society, it took some time for gardeners to find their appropriate place in the scheme of things. In most places, horticultural organizations were an offshoot of agricultural societies and had a formal relationship with the provincial departments of agriculture. In Ontario (then Upper Canada) as elsewhere, the provincial government supported the societies with grants.

Since 1854 horticultural societies themselves had been eligible for grants but only through the local agricultural society. In 1857, however, regulations for the horticultural societies were formalized. Two years later the Fruit Growers' Association was also formed. In order to establish a large distribution for its publication, which was called the *Canadian Horticulturist*, the Fruit Growers' Association included horticultural association members in its mailings. Soon, however, it became apparent that horticultural associations needed an independent organization to speak on their behalf.

In 1906 the Ontario Horticultural Association was formed. It had a membership of sixty societies representing 2700 individuals, and grants were awarded directly to the societies based on their membership. At the same time, in order to protect them from being taken over, these horticultural groups were excluded from exhibiting with the agricultural societies: "As past experience has shown, if there is a loophole left open, the Agricultural societies are going to try and get hold of funds of Horticultural societies."[7]

As early as 1860 the Ontario government's Board of Agriculture had been actively encouraging home gardening: "Landscaping and kitchen gardening, we fear, do not secure the attention to which their importance entitles them. A well laid out and carefully cultivated garden ranks among the highest efforts of

This historic plaque was unveiled in Allan Gardens in Toronto in recognition of the founding of the Toronto Horticultural Society in 1834, acknowledged as the first in Ontario.

Photograph by Jeremy Martin

artistic skill."[8] By 1878, however, D.W. Beadle, writing in the *Canadian Horticulturist*, could report a change:

> For a long time the only variety of vegetable enjoyed by the great proportion of our people was the potato. Very little attention was paid to the garden by our farmers, many of them had none at all; the only green peas were the poor, wretched things which were taken from the field—plundered from the swine, to which they properly belonged; and perhaps a few ears of green corn, in their season from the corn field. Rich, marrowfat peas, and sweet corn, were things almost unknown. It is very pleasant, indeed, to notice a growing inquiry for better vegetables, and more of them.[9]

Important as the *Canadian Horticulturist* was for farmers in particular, home gardeners still found information hard to come by. By 1900 subscribers were asking for more articles on flowers and vegetables: "We have not got one good *gardening* magazine in Canada that I know of," wrote one.[10]

FARTHER WEST

Across the prairies the CPR station gardens had a broader influence than elsewhere. As the only local source of garden expertise in many places, the stations became centres for information on gardening and on plants that would survive in the local climate. Railway employees were often members of the local horticultural society and were sometimes involved in getting them off the ground. The station itself was a useful meeting place in smaller centres, and the well-tended station gardens provided an incentive for improving the grounds around private homes. "Garden club activities of today have their roots in the annual bench shows, garden tours, plant sales, demonstrations and public services first promoted and offered by railway gardeners."[11]

In Manitoba, after a number of short-lived attempts to organize such groups as the Manitoba Forestry and Horticultural Society and the Manitoba Floral Association in the 1880s, the Manitoba Horticultural Association was started in 1895 and later expanded to a prairie organization. The Calgary Horticultural Society was formed in 1908 with the aim of "making Calgary a city beautiful, not only in name, but in fact." Ninety years later, the group was able to celebrate a long history with pride in what had been accomplished. Local horticultural societies sprang up throughout the

J.R. Almey, chief horticulturist for the CPR from 1929 to 1960, was also a leading figure in the horticultural associations for both Winnipeg and Manitoba.

Canadian Pacific Archives/A.20639

west in the early decades of the century, and by 1930 there were fifty organizations across the prairies.

By then horticultural societies and garden clubs were forming throughout the country. In Nova Scotia, for instance, they were all garden clubs, and the Nova Scotia Association of Garden Clubs was organized in 1935. In some cases, the activities of the clubs and societies were much the same. In others, the horticultural societies were mainly interested in fruit and vegetable growing. The organizers were men, although women were usually involved in the societies as well. Women were more directly involved in the organization and running of some of the garden clubs that were devoted to flower growing, such as the Garden Club of Toronto, which first met in 1947. In 1954 a federation called Garden Clubs of Ontario was created.

GETTING TO WORK

The horticultural societies and their councils, as well as the garden clubs, took their responsibility for beautifying the landscape very seriously. They often undertook work that might reasonably be considered the responsibility of government. Major H.J. Snelgrove, president of the Ontario Horticultural Society, spoke passionately of this at the 1908 annual meeting:

If we are to provide a revulsion against untidy streets, hideous alleys, tumble-down houses, repulsive garbage heaps, offensive advertising of black and yellow on dead walls and mountainsides, we must become teachers of beauty. Against these gross abuses of the senses of sight and smell, our school children should be taught to wage strenuous warfare.[12]

Across the country, members planted trees along the highways and at the schools. They grew vegetables in vacant lots and provided food to the needy. They cleaned up neglected cemeteries and planted them with shrubs and flowers, and laid out and maintained flower beds in public places. Members distributed plants, bulbs and seeds (including seeds for children), awarded prizes for the best gardens, and organized drives to rid the streets and yards of garbage. They also organized exhibitions of plants and flowers and, of course, gave talks and lectures on plants and gardens. "By the early 1900s many Societies were active in street tree planting, park planting and general horticultural beautification and were taking over the maintenance of some parks, as they did in Belleville in 1912."[13] Individuals such as W.W. Ashley, a member of the Saskatoon Horticultural Society and one of the founders of the Saskatchewan Horticultural

Society, took it upon himself to distribute elm seed packages all across the country.

In 1930 a countrywide campaign was undertaken to beautify the nation's homes and public spaces. The Canadian Horticultural Council, in co-operation with the Department of Agriculture in Ottawa, published a pamphlet entitled *Beautifying the Home Grounds of Canada*. In the preface W.T. Macoun, who was then on the executive of the Canadian Horticultural Council, wrote:

> There is much interest in the beautification of home surroundings in Canada. Never in the history of the Dominion was the desire as great to make the home attractive as it is to-day, and everything possible should be done to encourage those, who have this desire, to carry out some good plan.
>
> There are so many things in modern life to lessen the influence of the home that it needs something to make it more and more attractive in order to hold and increase the attachment to this important centre of national life, hence the planting of the grounds commends itself to parents who know the value of making their homes as attractive as possible for their children.[14]

Fairs grew out of early markets, where there always seemed to be competitions for the biggest and best. Although there were fairs in the country as early as the eighteenth century, they really came into their own in the second half of the nineteenth. Displays of fruit and vegetables dominated, but flowers were there as well. In spite of a somewhat contentious beginning, horticultural associations, agricultural associations and fairs are aware of how important they are to each other and have maintained a close working relationship.

Archives of Ontario/RG 16–274 AO 4823

Huge crowds visit the displays and sales that many botanical gardens and garden clubs make available in the spring, such as Victoria's Art in Bloom, Saskatoon's Gardenscape Outdoor Living Show, and the Flower, Plant and Garden Show at Place Bonaventure in Montreal. The largest is Toronto's Canada Blooms, seen here in 2000, where more than 100,000 visitors had a chance to see the latest garden trends and make plans for the coming season.

Canada Blooms: The Toronto Flower and Garden Show/Photograph by Tony Bock

As well as encouraging home landscaping, the campaign included the planting of ornamental trees, shrubs and flowering plants on public land.

"Horticultural Societies and Garden Clubs are contributing to the Horticultural well-being of our Country," noted Leslie Laking, director of the Royal Botanical Gardens in Hamilton, in an address given in 1967 to the International Horticultural Congress. "Their influence has been widely felt, particularly in the past 20 years, where it has resulted in a new awareness of the importance of well kept home properties, and has overflowed into development and beautification of public lands and public buildings."[15] He went on to praise their influence in the development of botanical gardens and arboreta.

All across the country when summer comes, local societies, small and large, host flower shows, such as Flowerama in Tweed, Ontario.

Photograph by Terry DaSilva

By the end of the twentieth century, the interest in gardening had grown and so had the number of garden clubs and horticultural societies. The Ontario Horticultural Society had 375 associations and 45,000

The Master Gardener program, originally developed in Washington State, operates in four Canadian provinces—British Columbia, Alberta, Saskatchewan and Ontario. Interested gardeners are trained as master gardeners who are then responsible for making gardening information available in their neighbourhoods and, in particular, for answering gardening questions from the general public.

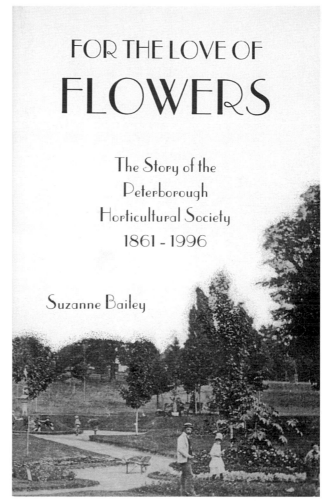

FOR THE LOVE OF
FLOWERS

The Story of the
Peterborough
Horticultural Society
1861 - 1996

Suzanne Bailey

In recent years many horticultural societies have published the story of their role in the history of Canadian gardening.

Peterborough Horticultural Society, 1996

members. Describing how valuable local garden clubs have become in the Atlantic provinces, Carol Matthews wrote, "This isn't the white-gloves and tea crowd of a few decades ago." They get their hands dirty! Calling garden clubs one of the fastest growing organizations in the Atlantic region, she continued, "There are more than 50 clubs in Nova Scotia alone, and New Brunswick has a least a dozen. The Garden Club of Prince Edward Island, one of several in the province, has more than 200 members; while in Newfoundland the St. John's-based hort society has satellite clubs in smaller towns across the province."[16]

The story is much the same in the rest of the country, where there are few serious gardeners who don't have some place where they can meet and discuss their adventures in the garden. ❧

7
Gardens of
Learning and Delight

THE FARM

Farming was of enormous importance in peoples' lives as well as to the economy of the country during the second half of the nineteenth century (it was estimated that more than 80 per cent of the Canadian population still made their living from the land at the end of the century). Important though agriculture was, practical advice for farmers was difficult to come by. There were useful publications such as *Journal d'agriculture*, *Family Herald* and *The Farmer's Advocate*, but there was no specific place where farmers could look for knowledgeable advice on how to improve their methods or

what the best seeds were for their growing conditions. In 1886, after much study of what should be done to give more support to farmers, the government of Sir John A. Macdonald brought in the Experimental Farm Station Act to establish five experimental farms across the country. These stations carried out research in all areas of agriculture and worked with farmers and gardeners to test and breed plants to develop those that would do best in the different climates and conditions across the country.

The first step was to create the Central Experimental Farm on 188 hectares on the outskirts of Ottawa (today well within city boundaries). The Experimental Farm, welcomed with great enthusiasm, was described by many as "almost a national park." It soon became affectionately known in the city simply as "the Farm." Its first director was William Saunders, one of those brilliant, passionate individuals to whom so many of the country's early institutions owe their success. Saunders had started his working life as an apprentice druggist, and

---

A rhododendron (*Rhododendron oreodoxa*), glowing in the mist, is typical of the many varieties found in the David C. Lam Asian Garden at the University of British Columbia Botanical Garden.

University of British Columbia Botanical Garden/Photograph by June West

This impressive house in the then-popular "shingle style" design was built for the director, William Saunders, and his family in the first years after the Central Experimental Farm was established in 1886. The house was demolished and replaced by the William Saunders Building in 1936. This photograph was taken in November 1898.

National Archives of Canada/PA-028041

that led him to take an interest in the insects that attacked many of the plants then used in drugs. He went on to help found the Entomological Society of Canada. At the same time, Saunders, an avid gardener, was involved in introducing a number of new varieties of fruit, as well as serving as president of the Fruit Growers' Association of Ontario.

Saunders threw himself energetically into creating Canada's experimental farm system. Not only did he manage to get things underway in Ottawa, but he also travelled across the country to establish four other farms, at Nappan in Nova Scotia, Brandon in Manitoba, Indian Head in Saskatchewan (then the Northwest Territories) and Agassiz in British Columbia. His wife, Agnes, was often left behind to entertain the many visitors that the new Central Experimental Farm attracted. Before long, new varieties of seeds were being developed in the Farm's horticultural division, and samples of seeds and plants were being shipped across the country to growers willing to raise test crops.

In July 1887 James Fletcher, another entomologist who understood how important the study of insects was to farmers, joined the Experimental Farm staff in Ottawa. A few years later he presented his personal collection of more than 3000 mounted plant specimens to the Farm's new herbarium. He also organized an arboretum and had twenty-six hectares set aside for woody plants and trees. Fletcher is well remembered for his role in starting the Ottawa Field Naturalists' Club in 1879. The Fletcher Wildlife Garden at the Central Experimental Farm is named for him.

In the Experimental Farm's horticulture division, more than a thousand varieties of apple, plum, pear and other fruit trees, as well as fruit-bearing shrubs and strawberries, were gathered from northern countries around the world and tested for their potential in Canada. Before the end of the nineteenth century, the Farm was able to recommend the varieties of fruits best suited to each region of the country and provide detailed information on such specific questions as how best to store apples and how to prune grapes.

In 1889 W.T. Macoun was appointed head of the Experimental Farm's horticulture division. (He was the son of John Macoun, the Dominion Botanist whose plant-collecting exploits are described in chapter 2.) He established what eventually became a national system of arboreta of native and introduced

A garden party held on the grounds of the Central Experimental Farm in Ottawa in June 1905.

National Archives of Canada/PA-042306

One of the favourite times to visit the Central
Experimental Farm was during the chrysanthemum show,
which started in 1912. Because of funding cuts, it was
discontinued in 1994. This lush photo was taken in the
1920s as a Farm worker prepares one of the greenhouses
for the show.

National Archives of Canada/PA-043244

104

species, first in Ottawa, then across the country. Under Macoun, the noted plant hybridist Isabella Preston was hired. (Her award-winning work is described in chapter 8.)

One of William Saunders's most important innovations was the development of a wheat-breeding program. His son Charles became head of the Farm's experimental section and was responsible for the development of Marquis wheat in the first decade of the twentieth century. By 1920, 90 per cent of the spring wheat grown in western Canada and 60 per cent grown in the United States was Marquis. Soon Canada was famous throughout the world for this hard wheat, which became the international standard for making bread.

Over the next fifty years, branches, laboratories, stations and substations of the experimental farm system developed, until a broad network existed right across the country. Many were set up in small communities. They attracted people with up-to-date knowledge and provided employment and valuable information for the towns, the farmers and the gardeners in the region. After the Second World War, two research stations were set up in the north, one in the Yukon and one at Fort Simpson in the Northwest Territories. They were both closed in 1970 after having completed their assessment of the regions. A station was later opened at Fort Chimo in northern

The superintendent's residence at the Lethbridge station in 1908 and the same house in 1936 showing the transformation from the bald prairie.

One of the biggest problems facing farmers on the prairies was soil erosion as winds swept across the flat landscape. The fields of grain at the experimental stations were planted between shelter belts of trees, producing attractive rows of trees and sturdy crops. As seen here, prairie homes also benefited from the protection of trees.

Fifty Years of Progress on Dominion Experimental Farms: 1886-1936 (Ottawa: Department of Agriculture, 1936), 140

Macoun Memorial Garden with its central pond is a favourite place for wedding photos. It opened in 1936, marking the Central Experimental Farm's fiftieth anniversary.

Photograph by Malak Ottawa

Quebec, but the difficulties of growing vegetables that far north were so severe that it was closed in 1965.

BOTANICAL GARDENS

Botanical gardens and arboreta (gardens devoted to woody plants and trees) usually combine scientific, educational and recreational purposes. "Each individual botanical garden will find that it has a different position on the continuum between private and pub-

lic programs, between regional and world habitats, between dedication to botany and pleasure for the public."[1]

Although the Central Experimental Farm is sometimes referred to as Canada's oldest botanical garden, with its plant development work over the decades and its beautiful garden beds, it has never been designated as a botanical garden (its garden beds are described as "an ornamental garden"). But there are now many more such specialized gardens devoted to

106

The earliest botanical gardens appeared in Islamic Spain in the tenth century in response to an intense interest in ornamental gardens, in gardening generally and in everything to do with plants, including their medicinal uses. More than 500 years passed before a similar interest developed in western Europe. During the Renaissance, the first botanical garden was established in Padua, Italy (where it can still be seen). It is considered to be the beginning of botanical gardens as we know them today. From Italy the idea spread throughout the rest of Europe, as did the study of botany, which was stimulated by the discovery of new plants from around the world during the great Age of Exploration.

the scientific study of plant life and the enjoyment of nature's beauty. The Directory of Canadian Botanical Gardens and Arboreta lists nearly eighty of these scientific gardens, large and small, from the Memorial University of Newfoundland Botanical Garden at Oxen Pond in St. John's to the Yukon Botanical Garden in Whitehorse.

Some of the largest and most beautiful botanical gardens and arboreta in the world can be found in Canada. It is impossible for any one garden to grow and display all of the plants of the world or to foster serious studies in every possible area. But many of Canada's botanical gardens have carved out a special area for themselves, often based on the climate and geography of their location.

LE JARDIN BOTANIQUE DE MONTRÉAL

One of Canada's most impressive botanical gardens is Le Jardin botanique de Montréal (Montreal Botanical Garden), established in 1931. The idea of creating a botanical garden for Quebec had come and gone twice during the nineteenth century. It seemed likely, therefore, that another attempt at the height of the Depression in 1929 would also fail. No doubt it would have if not for the tenacity of one man, Frère Marie-Victorin, the botanist and teacher who contributed so much to the study of plant life in Quebec (his work is described in chapter 2).

After returning from an extended trip to Africa and Europe, Marie-Victorin launched a campaign for a botanical garden in Montreal:

> I have come back filled with the need for a city like ours and a university like that of Montreal to have a large, scientifically organized, botanic garden, where students and amateurs alike may experience the pure

The impressive Jardin botanique de Montréal is one of three science institutions located together in Montreal.

Photograph by Malak, Ottawa

Frère Marie-Victorin with students in the children's garden at Le Jardin botanique de Montréal.

Le Jardin botanique de Montréal

and personal joy of a great garden, where God's great marvels are united for science and for art.[2]

There were a number of setbacks and disagreements over the years that followed, but the idea prevailed. Marie-Victorin was supported in his efforts by Louis Dupire, a journalist who championed the idea in the press, and Henry Teuscher, the landscape architect who designed the garden. Finally, in 1931, Le Jardin botanique de Montréal was opened to the public.

Today this garden presents a microcosm of the world of plants: "With its collection of 26,000 plant species and varieties, 10 exhibition greenhouses and some 30 thematic gardens, [it] is undeniably one of the loveliest botanical gardens in the world."[3] In recent years it has become home to three impressive science institutions: the Biodome showing the four complete ecosystems of the Americas, the Insectarium with its diverse display of live and mounted entomological collections, and the Botanical Garden itself.

THE ROYAL BOTANICAL GARDENS

The largest botanical garden in the world is in Hamilton, Ontario. The Royal Botanical Gardens first opened to the public in 1932, shortly after Le Jardin botanique de Montréal opened (the designation "Royal" came nine years later). The 1100 hectares of the gardens are located at the west end of Lake Ontario on a magnificent site that includes marshes and wetlands, rocky escarpments, forests, rolling hills and wilderness areas with nearly fifty kilometres of nature trails. This richly diverse landscape lies at the northern edge of the Carolinian forest (the gardens are on the same latitude as the French Riviera) and includes plants and trees normally found only to the

Work on the Royal Botanical Gardens began in 1929 as a relief project during the Depression. The remains of abandoned sand and gravel pits became the first garden—a beautiful, hidden amphitheatre of spring-flowering bulbs—seen here before and after.

Royal Botanical Gardens, Hamilton, Ontario

Centre for Canadian Historical Horticultural Studies, Royal Botanical Gardens, Hamilton, Ontario

In 1947 Leslie and Barbara Laking started the Children's Garden as part of the Royal Botanical Gardens' educational program. It was designed to introduce children to the pleasure of plants and gardening. Over the years, adult programs were added, allotment gardens were created for the community and gardening as therapy was introduced. Renamed the Teaching Garden, in the 1990s its activities were assumed by the city.

Centre for Canadian Historical Horticultural Studies, Royal Botanical Gardens, Hamilton, Ontario

south of Canada. The Cootes Paradise Marsh of 480 hectares, half of it freshwater shallows, has been a wildlife refuge since 1927. A restoration program undertaken in the 1990s will eventually recreate a self-sustaining ecosystem, complete with native plants and game-fish spawning grounds. The eighty hectares lying along the Niagara Escarpment, treasured for its birds and animals as well as its breathtaking spring waterfalls, are part of the UNESCO World Biosphere Reserve.

The cultivated gardens are divided into five separate areas. The Rose Garden includes an astonishing array of roses, as well as individual gardens devoted to medicinal plants, lilies, herbs and clematis. The Arboretum features a wide variety of native trees and shrubs and a world-famous collection of lilacs. The Laking Garden was named for Leslie Laking, director of the Royal Botanical Gardens from 1954 to 1981, and his wife, Barbara, who was active in the work of the Gardens; it contains a series of perennial beds and the Heritage Garden. In the Rock Garden spring bulbs are highlighted. The central building houses a greenhouse, where scientific and educational studies take place, and includes a reference library with the best collection of historical seed catalogues and horticultural publications in the country.

The peat beds of Memorial University of Newfoundland Botanical Garden present a colourful display with more than 200 varieties of plants, including heathers, rhododendrons, blueberries and a host of other native flowering plants.

Memorial University of Newfoundland Botanical Garden

MEMORIAL UNIVERSITY OF NEWFOUNDLAND BOTANICAL GARDEN

A few kilometres from the Atlantic Ocean on the Avalon Peninsula lies the most easterly botanical garden in Canada and one of the newest. The Memorial University of Newfoundland Botanical Garden has been open to the public only since 1977. With over forty hectares of forest, barrens, bogs and fens surrounding Oxen Pond, there is plenty of room for a wide variety of display gardens, which include a rock garden and individual gardens devoted to rhododendrons, flowers for drying, vegetables and heritage plants collected from the gardens of early settlers.

The trails, which retain their offbeat historical names (Hangman's Path, Soldier's Droke, Governor's Path), lead through a coniferous forest, past woodland wildflowers and blankets of mosses and lichens, past Oxen Pond and through a fen. The gardens feature indigenous plants and trees, as well as non-native varieties that thrive in the local climate.

Peat is a dominant feature of the Newfoundland environment, and the Botanical Garden's peat beds, built from locally cut peat blocks, support over 200 varieties of plants, including the white *Rhododendron canadense*, Labrador tea (*Ledum groenlandicum*), the showy lady's slipper (*Cypripedium reginae*) and the carnivorous pitcher plant (*Sarracenia purpurea*), the province's floral emblem.

111

THE UNIVERSITY OF BRITISH COLUMBIA BOTANICAL GARDEN

John Davidson was a Scottish botanist and artist who arrived in British Columbia about 1911, just in time to be appointed provincial botanist and to begin work on the newly created garden just east of Vancouver. The provincial government's aim was to collect plants from all parts of the province so they could be identified and studied. By 1916 Davidson had overseen the collection of 9000 species, with the help of an army of teachers, surveyors, ranchers and prospectors. The plant collection was moved to the campus of the new University of British Columbia that year. Davidson contributed a great deal to botanical studies in the province. He was a prodigious collector and lecturer, he wrote extensively, and he enthusiastically supported educational projects. "As a botanical artist, Davidson produced clear illustrations intended to aid in understanding scientific concepts and features in a form readily accessible to the viewer."[4]

From this early start the Botanical Garden, under the direction of Davidson until 1951, grew to its present twenty-eight hectares with a worldwide collection of plants from temperate climates. In partnership with the B.C. Nursery Trades Association and the B.C. Society of Landscape Architects, the Botanical Garden initiated a unique program to identify and propagate the province's native plants for commercial use. Through the Plant Introduction Scheme, many of these plants have become available to home growers.

Dedicated to education and research, the U.B.C. Botanical Garden includes a number of special gardens, including the Alpine Garden, the Winter Garden, the Native Garden, the Physick Garden and the Food Garden. It is particularly proud of the Nitobe Memorial Garden, an authentic Japanese garden designed and supervised by Kannosuke Mori, a leading Japanese landscape architect.

THE VANDUSEN BOTANICAL GARDEN

In 1975 a Vancouver botanical garden was created after residents intervened when the CPR, owners of the property, proposed a subdivision on the open landscape of an abandoned golf course. The VanDusen Botanical Garden has something for everyone, from native plants to magnolias and magnificent rhododendrons. Plants from six continents are displayed in natural settings and arranged to illustrate botanical relationships. The mild Vancouver climate allows the gardens to be enjoyed all year round.

At the VanDusen Botanical Garden, the Laburnum Walk with its golden chains of blossoms is a favourite spot for many visitors. The walk leads to a perennial garden full of colourful flowers and ornamental grasses.

VanDusen Botanical Garden/Photograph by David Jones

DEVONIAN BOTANIC GARDEN

In its unique northern location, just south of Edmonton, the University of Alberta's Devonian Botanic Garden specializes in alpine and cold-hardy plants. It is one of the largest botanical gardens in Canada, with about thirty-six hectares of gardens and almost forty-five hectares of natural landscape. Many beautiful garden areas are maintained, including a subtropical butterfly house and the Native People's Garden, where the names of plants appear in Cree and Cree syllabics.

A recent innovative program at the Botanic Garden has led to the creation of a plant diversity

The Devonian Botanic Garden was established by the University of Alberta in 1959. Beautifully situated in an area of rolling hills just outside Edmonton, its eighty-seven hectares encompass a wide range of gardens and collections. The Kurimoto Japanese Garden, pictured here, is designed to harmonize with the natural landforms and vegetation of the site.

Devonian Botanic Garden

Although well-maintained trails pass through beautiful gardens at the University of Guelph's Arboretum, trees are its main focus. Its most important woody plant collections emphasize the native trees of Canada and include a gene bank "to preserve the genetic diversity of Ontario's rare woody plants and to produce seed for future restoration work." Among the special activities the Arboretum has undertaken in recent years are the Ontario Tree Atlas Project and the Elm Recovery Project.

Photograph by Carol Martin

Most of the native prairie grasslands that once filled the southern parts of Alberta, Saskatchewan and Manitoba have been ploughed under and replaced by wheat. Winnipeg's Living Prairie Museum now maintains some of the original native grasses and flowers that once dominated the landscape.

Living Prairie Museum, Environmental Services Department, City of Winnipeg

centre for the prairie provinces and northern Canada. Here the Devonian will concentrate on identifying plants that are at risk before their numbers are compromised and developing a seed bank to ensure that both rare and common plants are saved for the future.

Many botanical gardens across the country specialize in unique features of the area in which they are situated; others have developed in response to a particular regional need. The Living Prairie Museum in Winnipeg, for example, retains a vestige of the grasslands that once covered the prairies. Some of Canada's botanical gardens have a long and fascinating history; others, such as the Fredericton Botanic Gardens, which opened in 1990, are just starting out. ❦

8
New Seeds for a New Land

Botanical interest in the nineteenth century had been focused for the most part on collecting and classifying plants and studying their distribution from region to region and around the world. In the following century, the emphasis shifted to the selective breeding of plants to encourage their most desirable or popular qualities. In Canada this meant developing strains that could survive in the country's often inhospitable climate.

Home gardeners, particularly in the early days, were the first plant breeders. They saved seeds from their best plants each year and gradually improved the varieties and developed their own strains through selection. Many of these individual varieties have been lost, but some were eventually forwarded to testing stations and saved. "Unfortunately the ability to select was seldom accompanied by a recording system. Thus many good selected strains were never identified except in the memories of the home gardeners and immediate relatives and friends."[1]

Systematic plant breeding was first undertaken by interested amateurs and hobbyists. But after the establishment of the experimental farm stations in 1886, it was the Central Experimental Farm's horticulture division that organized experiments in plant breeding and hybridizing, and supported, stimulated and encouraged the work of others. There was a general feeling "that the growing of fruits and vegetables on all farms was both profitable and necessary for the well-being of the farm family."[2]

The development of Marquis wheat in 1909 was the Central Experimental Farm's first big success. It was followed by other wheat strains aimed at solving the problems of stem rust and the early frosts of the prairies. Over the following decades, strains of wheat

Isabella Preston, shown here with some of the lilies that made her famous.

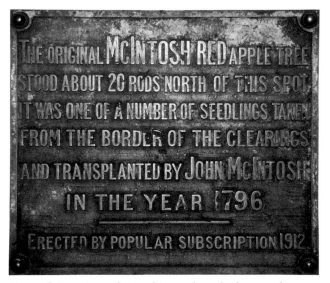

Few cultivars in gardening history have had as much impact as the McIntosh apple. In 1811 John McIntosh discovered that one of the seedlings on his farm at Dundela in southeastern Ontario bore particularly flavourful fruit. When his son learned how to graft, the family began producing apples and seedlings for sale. The McIntosh remains a popular eating apple, and the many strains developed over the years have become a major part of our most important fruit crop. The original tree lived until 1910, and the plaque shown here now marks its place.

Photograph by John T.A. Proctor

and other cereal crops were developed to respond to disease, the climate and the requirements of the market. Significant improvements were also made in other important commercial crops, such as rapeseed (canola), corn and potatoes.

From the very beginning, the development of hardy fruit varieties was central to the work of the Experimental Farm. Before his appointment as its first director, William Saunders had already been experimenting with fruit breeding at his home in London, Ontario. When he moved to Ottawa, he brought along hundreds of seedlings from his collection and continued his work at the Experimental Farm. His apple hybrids, based on the hardy Siberian crabapple, led to a number of varieties of crabapples and larger, good-quality apples that would survive on the prairies. Saunders is also credited with introducing the caragana (*Caragana arborescens*), or Siberian pea tree, to the prairies, where it became an important shelter-belt standard.

Following Saunders's retirement in 1911, W.T. Macoun, Dominion Horticulturist, continued the Farm's apple-breeding work. By 1926 he had named 174 varieties, many of them crosses with McIntosh, including such familiar names as Lobo, Melba and Joyce.

Experimental stations across the country were also hybridizing apples, which became one of Canada's most important crops. In Kentville, Nova Scotia, an orchard of more than 30,000 trees was established as high-quality fruit with resistance to rust was developed. At Morden in Manitoba, W.R. Leslie, an enthusiastic horticulturist who was superintendent of the station for thirty-five years, developed varieties particularly suited to the Canadian prairies and the northern United States. And he was instrumental in creating the Prairie Cooperative Fruit Breeding Project, working with the universities of Saskatchewan and Alberta and the Alberta Department of Agriculture. The Summerland Station in British Columbia was particularly successful with Spartan apples. In 1936 they were "voted the best-tasting apples at English fruit shows."[3] Over the decades, successful new varieties of such fruit as cherries, strawberries, raspberries, Saskatoon berries and, in more recent times, hardy kiwi fruit have all been bred to thrive in the Canadian climate.

Roses, so loved by gardeners around the world and so difficult to overwinter in our climate, became a special project at the Experimental Farm. In 1900 Saunders bred the cultivar 'Agnes' (*Rosa rugosa* x *R. foetida* 'Persiana'), still a popular rose today. Three floribunda roses were introduced from the Morden research station in the 1960s and 1970s: 'Assiniboine,' 'Cuthbert Grant' and 'Adelaide Hoodless.' The most popular recent hybrids are the Canadian Explorer roses. The creations of Felicitas Svejda at the Central

In 1882 Albert Edward McKenzie moved with his family from Ontario to Brandon, Manitoba. When his father died, McKenzie took over the family's feed and flour business and started devoting himself to supplying seeds to the growing population. The company's first complete seed catalogue was sent out in 1900. This century celebration seed package repeats a design used in 1906, with a foxglove illustration from 1901. Today A.E. McKenzie Co. (including the McFayden and McConnell seed companies) remains proud that "no other company has put as many vegetables on Canadian dining tables, nor decorated as many homes and farms with shrubs and flowers."[4]

119

'William Baffin' (a *Rosa kordesii* hybrid), one of the Explorer series of roses developed by Felicitas Svejda at the Central Experimental Farm's Research Station in Ottawa. Explorer roses are popular for their winter-hardy, disease-resistant qualities and for their showy flower clusters.

Agriculture and Agri-Food Canada

Experimental Farm, all the roses in this series are extremely hardy, full of rose clusters and tend to flower over a long period of time. "More than 150 varieties have been introduced by Canadian breeders since the 1890s; only one-quarter are of the tender sort, the remainder are hardy."[5]

ISABELLA PRESTON AND HER FLOWERING PLANTS

One of the most fascinating people in Canadian plant breeding history is Isabella Preston. She was recognized as a key figure in the hybridizing of lilies not only in this country but in botanical circles around the world. Isabella Preston was born in England, the youngest daughter in a family of gardeners. She was thirty-one when she followed her sister to Guelph, Ontario. Isabella had always gardened, and when she arrived in Canada she decided to pursue her hobby by enrolling at the Ontario Agricultural College (now part of the University of Guelph). Horticulture was still an unusual field for a woman, but within a year she was working under the head of the department, J.W. Crow, first tending his plant experiments and later supervising the greenhouses.

Information on plant hybridizing and the discoveries of Gregor Mendel weren't formally introduced to gardeners and botanists until the end of the nineteenth century, so many of the hybridists in the early decades of the twentieth century were self-taught, including Isabella Preston. She read widely in her field and eventually took the lily as her special subject. The lily, although an ancient and well-known plant, was not the popular home garden flower it has since become. The success of her efforts was evident

Isabella Preston with some of the popular, late-flowering lilacs she developed while working at the Central Experimental Farm in Ottawa.

Centre for Canadian Historical Horticultural Studies, Royal Botanical Gardens, Hamilton, Ontario

as early as 1919 when the hybrid *Lilium* x *princeps* (a cross of *L. regale* and *L. sargentiae*) was made available to the public as 'George C. Creelman.' The plant was immediately recognized as a breakthrough.

By 1920 Preston was working at the Central Experimental Farm under W.T. Macoun. At the Farm there had always been interest in providing ornamental

121

Field Horse-tail   Plate III.
a-Sterile stem.
b-Fertile   "

Pasque Flower   Plate XIV.

Faith Fyles worked as a botanist and botanical artist at
the Central Experimental Farm from 1920 to 1931. In 1920
she wrote and illustrated *Principal Poisonous Plants of
Canada*. These two illustrations from the book show both
her accuracy and her artistic skill.

National Library of Canada

122

plants to beautify Canadian homes, and now here was someone who could dedicate herself to the task. (Typically for the time, Macoun had tried in vain to hire a man.) Macoun set Preston working with a challenging range of plant genera: lilies (where she had already achieved notable success), roses, lilacs, Siberian irises, columbines and crabapples. She devoted herself primarily to these plants until her retirement in 1948.

Preston had an admirable talent for naming the various cultivars of the species she specialized in. Her Siberian irises carried the names of Canadian rivers; the 'Ottawa' and 'Gatineau' irises were particularly successful. Her later lily cultivars, known as the "stenographer lilies," were named after the seven stenographers in the department. Her Rosybloom crabapples, with their fragrant, colourful blossoms, were named after Canadian lakes—'Athabasca,' 'Simcoe' and 'Scugog,' for example. Her lilacs won international acclaim for their size, their heavy blooms and their late-blooming quality. Though not award winners, her *Rosa rugosa* hybrids were more suitable for the cold Canadian winters than imported roses. Only her columbines were relatively unsuccessful. Altogether, Preston's work as a hybridizer was an extraordinary achievement.

As new hybrids are created, many of the original varieties are left behind. "Plant breeding is an ephemeral art," writes Edwinna von Baeyer in an essay on Isabella Preston's life. "A selected few of her crabapples still bloom at the Experimental Farm. A couple of her Siberian Iris continue to be sold by nurserymen. Her lilacs survive in home gardens and the catalogues of a few nurseries. But her 'crown,' her lilies, have nearly disappeared from private gardens and commercial distribution."[6] Preston's work, however, has been the basis for much of the later new cultivars of these species, and their descendants survive as some of the favourite plants in today's gardens.

FRANK LEITH SKINNER AND THE MANITOBA HARDY PLANT NURSERY

One of the most honoured plant breeders in the Canadian west was Frank L. Skinner. Skinner and his family immigrated to Manitoba from Scotland in 1895, when he was thirteen. Even as a very young boy, he had taken a keen interest in growing things. Unfortunately, the family's new homestead near Dropmore was in the northern part of the province (in zone 2) where few flowers or vegetables grew.

In 1901, while still a teenager, Skinner contacted the Central Experimental Farm for information on the trees and shrubs he was trying to establish on his family's farm. Eight years later he travelled to the

Manitoba Horticultural Society convention in Winnipeg where his extensive plant-growing knowledge didn't go unnoticed. The next year Skinner was invited to present a paper at the convention, and many more were to follow. Skinner's plan to continue as a rancher and farmer with his brother on their half section in Dropmore was interrupted when he was sent to Vancouver to convalesce from an illness. There he immersed himself in horticultural studies. When he returned to Dropmore, he was encouraged to turn his horticultural hobby into a business, and the Dropmore Hardy Plant Nursery was born in 1925.

The rest of Skinner's life was devoted to developing varieties of trees, shrubs and flowers that would flourish in the landscape he loved so well. He was in close touch with most of the significant botanical and horticultural figures of the period, as well as with botanical gardens in North America, Europe and Asia, where he found many of the species he developed for the prairies. "Here on the prairies," he wrote, "we have no native species of Apple, Pear or Lilac but all three of this genus of plants have species that grow wild in eastern Asia where the climate is at least as cold in winter as it is in western Canada." He introduced more than 200 hybrids to Canada; 144 were new or improved varieties. Among the most famous were a favourite honeysuckle, the Dropmore Scarlet

W.J. Boughen, with some of the fruit trees he developed for Boughen Nurseries near Neepawa in Manitoba. Boughen moved to the prairies from Ontario in 1891, bringing with him a love of flowers, trees and fruits. Within a few years he had transplanted wild fruit into his garden. This was the beginning of Boughen Nurseries; its first catalogue was printed in 1912. He was a dedicated plantsman and became Horticultural Explorer for Canada in 1920. The nursery is operated by the current generation of Boughens.

Boughen Nurseries Valley River Ltd.

Trumpet (*Lonicera* x *brownii* 'Dropmore Scarlet'), and the Dropmore lilies. (Rumour has it that there was a certain amount of competition between Skinner and Isabella Preston over the years.)

Skinner wrote widely and urged such improvements as plant patents for hybridists and the labelling of plants by place of origin. He was honoured with many awards for his pioneering work, including the M.B.E. he received on the recommendation of the Canadian government. After Skinner died in 1967, his family established the Frank Skinner Arboretum Trail near his old property. And at Skinner's Nursery, plant breeders continue to test and supply plants suitable for zone 2.

ROSCOE FILLMORE AND HIS MARITIME RHODODENDRONS

Roscoe Fillmore was a fifth generation Canadian, an ardent social activist and a lifetime horticulturist. Raised on a small pioneer farm in Albert County, New Brunswick, he never forgot the poverty and sickness his family had suffered during his early years. Ross (as the family called him) spent much of his life working to improve the lives of working people.

As a teenager in 1902, Ross began working at the Albert Nursery, which was famous throughout east-ern Canada and the United States for its apple trees. Soon he was learning the intricacies of creating an orchard and perfecting the technique of grafting. After recovering from an illness, he travelled across the country, took part in the harvest excursions and worked for the CPR. In 1907 he spent a year at Brown Brothers, a large and famous nursery in Rochester, New York. Here he expanded his knowledge of plants and their care. He was fascinated by the rhododendrons he saw arriving from Europe and noticed their similarity to the wild shrubs that bloomed in Albert County. It seemed to him that the European varieties could be hybridized to grow in the colder climate of the Maritimes, an idea he never forgot. "Roscoe's infatuation with rhododendrons and azaleas lasted a lifetime."[7]

When war came in 1914, Fillmore was manager of the largest commercial orchard in New Brunswick. Bitterly opposed to the war, he joined the Communist Party and travelled to Russia to help establish a commercial garden for the new revolutionary government. There were no prospects of a job when he returned to Canada, so he decided to start his own nursery on about one and a half hectares in Nova Scotia's fertile Annapolis Valley. Facing an excellent export market for apples at the time, he planted 2000 apple trees and leased a small local orchard. When the apple market fell apart, Fillmore concentrated on a wider variety of seedlings, shrubs, annuals and perennials. Pansies became the specialty of The Valley Nurseries. Before long, Fillmore discovered why there were few nurseries in Nova Scotia:

> The climate of the region was the despair of horticulturists. In winter much of the coldest weather came when there was no snow cover to help protect plants; and in summer there was often a prolonged hot, dry spell. To fight these conditions Roscoe set out to develop his own line of plants, carrying out extensive tests to determine which trees, shrubs and annuals would be adaptable to the Nova Scotia climate. Over the years he combed the countryside looking for hardy plants that he could grow from cuttings. One of the best sources was the federal government's experimental station at Kentville, where there were several hardy evergreens and trees.[8]

In 1938 Roscoe Fillmore became head gardener of the Dominion Atlantic Railways. His work involved caring for eight sites. One was the now-famous Grand Pré National Historic Park near Wolfville, which was created as a tribute to the Acadians who had been expelled in 1755. Some of the original willows planted by the Acadians and apple trees they had brought from France still survived. Roscoe turned the park into a showplace:

> Large bright-coloured beds of marigolds, petunias, and other annuals were planted to attract tourists. Shade trees were perfectly trimmed, and the lily ponds, where a flock of ducks spent the summer, were carefully groomed.[9]

During his later years Fillmore devoted much of his time to plant propagation. Through trial and error, weeding out plants that failed to survive the winter and breeding those that did, he developed hardy stocks and introduced many new species to the Atlantic region, particularly holly, magnolias, hydrangea and Colorado blue spruce. But it was with his best-loved rhododendrons and azaleas that he spent most of his time. Through his efforts, by the 1950s home gardeners were able to grow rhododendrons and azaleas throughout most of the Maritimes.[10]

Roscoe Fillmore wrote four books on gardening: *Green Thumbs: The Canadian Gardening Book*; *The Growing Question*; *The Perennial Border and Rock Garden*; and *Roses for Canadian Gardens*. They were published in the 1950s when there were very few books devoted to gardening in Canada. Not surprisingly, Fillmore's books were enthusiastically welcomed by Canadian gardeners.

During the first half of the twentieth century, many more individual growers and dedicated horticulturists were working in their own ways to develop hardy vegetables and flowering plants that would flourish in the extremes of the Canadian climate. They included Mary Eliza Blacklock of Rowancroft Gardens; Henry H. Groff and his prize gladiolus; Albert E. Brown of Sheridan Nurseries; W.R. Leslie of the Dominion Experimental Station at Morden, Manitoba; Spencer McConnell of McConnell Nursery; and Percy H. Wright of Saskatoon. According to garden writer Jennifer Bennett, "the gardener who is able to crack the code can find in seed names a mini-history of vegetable gardening, a revelation of horticulture's most exciting moments, a storehouse of hidden seed breeders' names and a layman's guide to marketing strategy."[11] Today vegetables must conform to an international code of nomenclature, and seed companies are no longer likely to reveal the names of the parent plants of their new cultivars.

The experimental farm research stations went on to become the Research Branch of Agriculture Canada, and eventually stations were established across the country. Most modern agricultural colleges and departments of agriculture at Canadian universities, farmer co-operatives and seed companies have plant breeding programs. And many home gardening enthusiasts continue to enjoy improving the flowers and vegetables in their gardens by crossing desirable plants or preserving the seeds of successful ones. 🐛

NUMBER TWENTY

$1.50

GG70413

Harrowsmith

Under The Aquadome: Solar Grown Trout And Vegetables
Time Warp At Kings Landing • Build A Nomadic Loom

THE CITY FARMERS

9
Back to the Land

WARTIME GARDENING

During both world wars, Canadian gardeners threw their energies behind the war effort in the area they knew best—the production of food. In 1917 the horticultural societies were proud of their efforts: "In this, the fourth year of the titanic struggle for the world's freedom, Ontario Horticultural Societies have succeeded in doing patriotic work in increased production of foodstuff through our garden efforts."[1] Vacant-lot gardening was expanded, and the ploughman's association contributed by preparing the beds. Even the railway station gardens became vegetable gardens to help out. All these efforts contributed hundreds of thousands of bushels of food for the cause. "[I]n a very real sense," wrote the *Canadian Horticulturist* in 1918, "the war may be won or lost in the fields, gardens, pastures and hog-lots of the North American continent."[2]

Twenty years later support was just as strong when the country once more went all out for the war effort. Women's Institutes urged women to do their part by raising as much food in their gardens as possible in order to leave commercially grown produce for overseas. Gardening advice, from planting ("Early fresh vegetables such as radish and lettuce may be had by sowing the seed in a hotbed early in April") to proper storage ("Find out how your neighbours store their vegetables, and write to the Extension Service for further Information"),[3] came from every level of government. Grounds around universities and government buildings were given over to growing vegetables, often with the unemployed doing the gardening. "Urged on by the government's pleas to 'Plant a Wartime Garden,' and aided by the city's decision to rent vacant land to horticulturists at a nominal fee, Victory Gardeners in Vancouver, New Westminster,

Harrowsmith, vol. 3, no. 8 (1979)

Ottawa's splendid Tulip Festival is one of the more unusual mementos of war. The Dutch Crown Princess, later Queen Julianna, was given sanctuary by Canada during the Second World War. While in Ottawa, her third child was born. At the war's end, the family returned home, and to show appreciation for Canada's wartime hospitality and its involvement in the liberation of Holland, the Princess sent 100,000 tulip bulbs to Ottawa. This was followed by a similar gift each year, to which the city added its own Dutch tulips. Over the years, the capitol has become world-renowned for its colourful annual tulip display.

Photograph by Malak, Ottawa

North and West Vancouver produced some 31,000 tons of fresh vegetables and fruits in the year 1943."[4]

When the Second World War finally ended in 1945, many of those who had been involved in the war effort returned from overseas or from wartime jobs within Canada anxious to get on with a more normal life. Marriages and births increased sharply over the following years. Young married couples were soon buying houses, many with the help of the Veterans' Land Act or other rehabilitation grants, and settling down to raise families. With new homes to landscape and a new appreciation of home-grown vegetables, gardening continued to be popular. In addition, the flood of refugees entering the country often brought their garden lore with them.

A NEW DECADE OF GARDENERS

It wasn't until the late 1960s and the 1970s that another social change lead to a fresh renewal of interest in home gardening. It came at a time when the population was increasing, the cities were expanding and supermarkets—with their mass-produced fruits and vegetables—were growing. Many people, missing the home-grown vegetables of their childhood, started small backyard gardens. Others decided to move back to the country. "It is a North American dream of 1970," wrote Alan Edmonds in *Maclean's* that year, "to escape the city, flee the rat race and get closer to the 'reality' of nature. The cautious who can afford it buy red-brick schoolhouses or farms. Others start communes which rarely survive even one summer."5

Just when a new decade of gardeners were seeking information, along came the publication of *Chatelaine's Gardening Book* in 1970. Written by Lois Wilson, its appearance was a seminal event in the story of garden publishing in Canada. Across the country, gardeners and garden experts enthusiastically welcomed Wilson's book for its simple, lively writing, its descriptions of growing conditions across the country, and its wealth of practical ideas, clear instructions and attractive illustrations. It was the first complete modern book on gardening in this country and was introduced just when Canadians were renewing their interest in backyard gardens and in beautifying the grounds around their homes. Its 380 pages are packed with information on every aspect of gardening, from lawns and trees to tools and techniques. Thirty years later, it continues to stand up very well.

Wilson's vegetable and flower advice covered every region of the country, including the north. She offered tips on growing flowers, vegetables, plants and trees in each region, and described how to establish specialized gardens for wildflowers, herbs or scented plants. She devoted one whole section to landscape planning. For many amateur gardeners, this was where they first saw a plant hardiness map for Canada with the zones from 0 to 9 clearly delineated. In writing the book, Wilson consulted with top horticulturists from across the country. *Chatelaine's Gardening Book* was as inclusive as such a book could be and remained the most important home-gardening reference work for the next twenty years.

When her book was published, Wilson was already an important figure in Canadian gardening circles. She was a well-known gardening writer and photographer. For nine years she was garden editor for *Chatelaine* magazine, where most of her gardening articles appeared. She was an active member of the Garden Club of Toronto, serving as its president from 1965 to 1967, and was closely involved in the creation

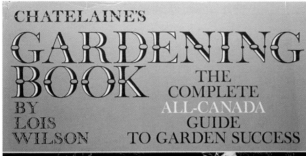

Chatelaine's Gardening Book was an important publication for Canadian gardeners when it first appeared in 1970. Written by Lois Wilson, the pre-eminent gardening authority of the day, with an expert body of consultants, its claim to be complete was entirely justified.

Lois Wilson, *Chatelaine's Gardening Book* (Toronto: Doubleday, 1970)

of two specialized gardens in the city, the Fragrant Garden for the blind and the Enchanted Garden for disabled children.

Although Wilson's articles had been appearing regularly in *Chatelaine* as well as in other magazines, such as *Canadian Homes and Gardens*, the subject of gardening attracted little general interest in the media. And *Canadian Homes and Gardens*, although popular in the 1950s in response to interest created by the postwar housing boom, was losing subscribers by the 1960s. It changed its name to *Canadian Homes* for a short time and then disappeared. Very few articles on the subject of gardening appeared during the 1960s, usually about one a year. By the 1970s this had begun to change.

In 1974 Marjorie Harris, who would go on to establish herself as a major gardening expert, published an article in *Chatelaine* that featured three five-year garden plans (including Lois Wilson's own garden). The *Financial Post* was beginning to report on a new gardening phenomenon in articles such as "Home Gardening Grows Like Topsy" on May 4, 1974. A major change in magazine publishing occurred in 1975 when the federal government enacted Bill C-58, which offered protection for Canadian magazines. This opened the way for the country to publish more of its own magazines rather than depending so heavily on the overflow from the United States. During the next two decades, new specialized publications began to appear, including a number directly related to gardening.

As for gardening books, statistics are less readily available. The explosion of cultural nationalism in the late 1960s, stimulated by the country's centennial in 1967, led to an increased interest in everything Canadian. Book publishers responded with a rash of new titles, and soon a number of new, small publishing houses sprang up across the country. In 1973 only twenty-six gardening book titles were available. They included Lois Wilson's book, of course, and titles by other garden experts of the period—Fred Dale, Stan Larke, Roscoe Fillmore—and one regional title, *The Prairie Gardener*, by Bert Harp. By 1980 the list had increased by nine titles, and more familiar names began to appear—Art Drysdale, Ken Reeves and David Tarrant. In Quebec, horticulturists such as Gaston Charbonneau were producing books in French.

THE SIMPLER LIFE

Immigration from the United States had a significant influence on gardening during this period and was related to the back-to-the-land movement, as people went in search of a simpler way of life. In *Americans*

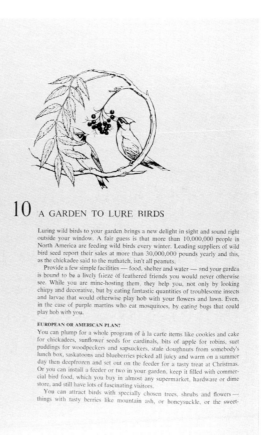

Lois Wilson, *Chatelaine's Gardening Book* (Toronto: Doubleday, 1970), 60

in *Canada: Migration and Settlement since 1840*, David Harvey has pointed out that during an earlier period Americans began to run out of wilderness in their own country and started to see Canada as a romantic place to escape from the aggravations of modern life. In the 1960s a rather different group of American immigrants flooded across the border, and they ended up influencing Canadian life in a variety

Jocelyn and David Harvey and their children lived off the land on the rock-strewn countryside north of Ottawa in the 1970s. They were part of a group of Americans who came to Canada during those years, some to escape the war in Vietnam, some looking for a simpler life. David went on to write *Americans in Canada: Migration and Settlement since 1840*.

Jocelyn Harvey

of cultural and social ways. They came for the most part because they objected to the war in Vietnam; many were draft dodgers. These expatriate Americans brought with them both a reaction against American mores and an ingrained American view of the world. Some were simply seeking a more natural way of life. They came here as homesteaders and often lived in small communal groups. They became part of a larger movement of Canadians who wanted to experience life closer to nature.

Country land was amazingly cheap at this time. In many areas the landscape was dotted with farms deserted by people moving to the growing cities. "If you've got $6,000 in the bank, a good job in the city and are on the prowl for a piece of country, you are far from unique," wrote Kathlyn Poff in a 1978 article entitled "The Good, the Bad and the Swampy." But, she went on to warn, "true homesteading involves a commitment that not one per cent of the population in North America would be able to keep."[6] The new settlers were serious about their attempts at subsistence farming, and some found it a satisfying, though often difficult, way of life.

Two magazines in particular sprang up in direct response to this interest. One began publication the year that *Chatelaine's Gardening Book* came out. Created at Rochdale College, a short-lived educational experiment in downtown Toronto, the *Canadian*

A page from the Spring 1971 issue of the *Canadian Whole Earth Almanac.*

Whole Earth Almanac was only in existence for three years, but it was one of the earliest responses to the back-to-the land, small-is-beautiful movement. This way of life affected only a relative few directly, but it became part of the general social movement that resulted in fields of garden plots in or near large cities and a new desire to see cities improved wherever possible by creating beauty with gardens.

The *Canadian Whole Earth Almanac*, inspired by the American *Whole Earth Catalogue,* was a self-help guide that advocated all kinds of projects that stressed self-reliance. Each of its irregularly published issues was more or less devoted to one general subject: food, shelter, wood, etc. The first issue, entitled "Food," emphasized very basic information that was not then readily available. The subjects were dear to the hearts of gardeners: organic gardening, mulching, companion planting, making a hot bed and creating windbreaks. There was even an article on how to establish a wild rice stand. The magazine offered potential homesteaders advice on how to find abandoned farms and cheap land, and was particularly valued as a resource for related information from a wide variety of sources, including the many publications available from the Canadian Department of Agriculture. The *Almanac* couldn't compete with regular consumer magazines for colour and general sophistication, but it had its own charm—simple cover designs printed in black and, inside, quaint illustrations (often reprinted from pioneer publications). It was packed with information from cover to cover.

Morninglory was one of the best-known homesteading co-operatives that grew up at that time. An article written for the *Almanac* by Marcia (first names were commonly used), one of its original settlers, captures the spirit of the movement:

> Once you've had some real food going into you for a while, it's hard to accept the make-believe stuff of stores. When you grow your own, you can get right into the cycle ... you get what you give. If you have built up the soil with compost and mulched the plants, they grow healthy and abundantly. When it comes time to harvest, you know them as friends ... The garden as a direct source of food becomes a tool directing us to simplicity.[7]

David Harvey describes this homesteading period as fairly short lived, from approximately 1968 to 1974, but it spawned and was encouraged by one of the most successful magazines in the country's history. *Harrowsmith* was the brainchild of James M. Lawrence, one of the expatriate Americans. Lawrence produced *Harrowsmith* along with what he described as "a ragtag group of unpaid, inexperienced publishing tyros." Working out of

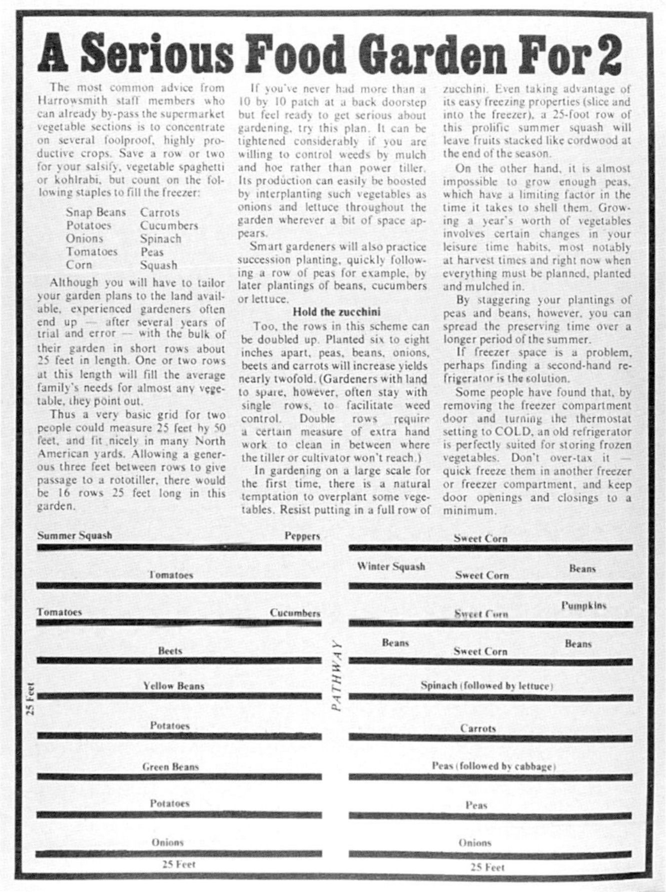

A Serious Food Garden For 2

The most common advice from Harrowsmith staff members who can already by-pass the supermarket vegetable sections is to concentrate on several foolproof, highly productive crops. Save a row or two for your salsify, vegetable spaghetti or kohlrabi, but count on the following staples to fill the freezer:

Snap Beans	Carrots
Potatoes	Cucumbers
Onions	Spinach
Tomatoes	Peas
Corn	Squash

Although you will have to tailor your garden plans to the land available, experienced gardeners often end up — after several years of trial and error — with the bulk of their garden in short rows about 25 feet in length. One or two rows at this length will fill the average family's needs for almost any vegetable, they point out.

Thus a very basic grid for two people could measure 25 feet by 50 feet, and fit nicely in many North American yards. Allowing a generous three feet between rows to give passage to a rototiller, there would be 16 rows 25 feet long in this garden.

If you've never had more than a 10 by 10 patch at a back doorstep but feel ready to get serious about gardening, try this plan. It can be tightened considerably if you are willing to control weeds by mulch and hoe rather than power tiller. Its production can easily be boosted by interplanting such vegetables as onions and lettuce throughout the garden wherever a bit of space appears.

Smart gardeners will also practice succession planting, quickly following a row of peas for example, by later plantings of beans, cucumbers or lettuce.

Hold the zucchini

Too, the rows in this scheme can be doubled up. Planted six to eight inches apart, peas, beans, onions, beets and carrots will increase yields nearly twofold. (Gardeners with land to spare, however, often stay with single rows, to facilitate weed control. Double rows require a certain measure of extra hand work to clean in between where the tiller or cultivator won't reach.)

In gardening on a large scale for the first time, there is a natural temptation to overplant some vegetables. Resist putting in a full row of zucchini. Even taking advantage of its easy freezing properties (slice and into the freezer), a 25-foot row of this prolific summer squash will leave fruits stacked like cordwood at the end of the season.

On the other hand, it is almost impossible to grow enough peas, which have a limiting factor in the time it takes to shell them. Growing a year's worth of vegetables involves certain changes in your leisure time habits, most notably at harvest times and right now when everything must be planned, planted and mulched in.

By staggering your plantings of peas and beans, however, you can spread the preserving time over a longer period of the summer.

If freezer space is a problem, perhaps finding a second-hand refrigerator is the solution.

Some people have found that, by removing the freezer compartment door and turning the thermostat setting to COLD, an old refrigerator is perfectly suited for storing frozen vegetables. Don't over-tax it — quick freeze them in another freezer or freezer compartment, and keep door openings and closings to a minimum.

Summer Squash
Peppers
Tomatoes
Tomatoes
Cucumbers
Beets
Yellow Beans
Potatoes
Green Beans
Potatoes
Onions
25 Feet
25 Feet
PATHWAY
Sweet Corn
Winter Squash
Sweet Corn
Beans
Sweet Corn
Pumpkins
Beans
Sweet Corn
Beans
Spinach (followed by lettuce)
Carrots
Peas (followed by cabbage)
Peas
Onions
25 Feet

A page from the first issue of *Harrowsmith*, published in 1976 and described on the cover as the "Spring Garden Issue." The article features a garden that grows enough basic vegetables to feed two people. It recommended that first-time gardeners "resist putting in a full row of zucchini."

Harrowsmith, vol. 1, no. 1 (1976): 8

an old farmhouse in the tiny village of Camden East northwest of Kingston, the group put together a magazine that struck just the right note by seizing the enthusiasm of this back-to-the-land movement.

Named after a village close to Camden East, *Harrowsmith* was almost literally an overnight success. Within two years it had over 100,000 subscribers and was one of the most popular magazines in the country. The small band of editors, all still in their twenties, were dedicated to the idea of living off the land themselves, and it shows in the magazine's earnest, enthusiastic spirit. But most of all, the content of the magazine in its early years was inspired. Its material was often supplied by the readers themselves. As Lawrence wrote: "Taking us at our word, [*Harrowsmith* readers] began banging down the doors with ideas, criticism, articles, photographs and demands that they be hired."

Along with numerous articles on wood stoves, alternative energy, homesteading, raising farm animals and living an ecologically sound life in general were a plethora of ideas and items on gardening. The very first issue included four articles on gardening. One described how to create a garden that would feed two people—what to plant, how much to plant and how to lay the garden out. Another advocated introducing blackberries to the home garden. "The Old Alchemists" tant than taste. Further, my decision to grow my own cabbage seed adds the requirement that the roots stay alive and frisky long enough that they can be planted in the garden the next spring and grow good seed.

A neighbour may rave about a huge squash, but will it keep well? Even if it does, perhaps you prefer several meal-sized squashes for your family. A tomato variety which ripens its fruit all at once is fine if you want a batch for home canning, but it's not so wonderful for prolonging the salad season. Such features are brought into sharp focus as you stand in front of a plant, recalling its performance through the entire season, debating if it should be a parent for your seeds.

In any row of vegetables one or more plants are likely to appear healthier and larger than the rest. These can be marked in some way, most easily by poking a marker stick next to the best specimens.

If, on the other hand, you are growing a field of something like beans just to propagate the seed, be sure to walk down the row and rogue out any inferior plants so that only the best will mature to produce seed.

It is essential that the seed grower know the reproductive cycle of any vegetable whose seed he hopes to save.

This may seem very basic to some gardeners, but if you expect to harvest beet seed, for example, the first year will be

---

SOME COMMON MEMBERS OF FOUR CUCURBITA SPECIES (THE SQUASH/PUMPKIN GROUP)
1. C. MAXIMA Buttercup Delicious Hubbard Mammoth
2. C. MIXTA Cushaw
3. C. MOSCHATA Butternut Crookneck Kentucky Field
4. C. PEPO Acorn Connecticut Field Cocozelle Delicata Jack-O-Lantern Lady Godiva Scallop Small Sugar Straightneck Vegetable Marrow Vegetable Spaghetti Zucchini

NOTE: Members of each species will pollinate each other. Some crosses might occur between species: 4 with 2 and 3; 1 with 3.

SELF-POLLINATING	
Beans Broad Beans Chicory Endive Lettuce Peas Tomato	*All are annuals or perennials treated as annuals in temperate zones*

CROSS-POLLINATING VEGETABLES (Including groups of vegetables which will pollinate one another)	GROWTH HABIT	POLLEN DISTRIBUTION
ASPARAGUS	Perennial	Insect
BEET GROUP		
Garden beet	Biennial	Wind
Mangel	Biennial	Wind
Sugar beet	Biennial	Wind
Swiss chard	Biennial	Wind
BRASSICA OLERACEA GROUP *		
Broccoli	Annual	Insect
Brussels sprouts	Biennial	Insect
Cabbage	Biennial	Insect
Cauliflower	Biennial	Insect
Collard	Biennial	Insect
Kale	Biennial	Insect
Kohlrabi	Biennial	Insect
BRASSICA, OTHER SPECIES *		
Chinese cabbage	Annual	Insect
Mustard	Annual	Insect
Radish	Annual	Insect
Rutabaga	Biennial	Insect
Turnip	Annual	Insect
CARROT	Biennial	Insect
CELERY	Biennial	Insect
CORN	Annual	Wind
CUCUMBER	Annual	Insect
EGGPLANT	Annual	Insect
MELON GROUP **		
Muskmelon	Annual	Insect
ONION	Biennial	Insect
PARSLEY	Biennial	Insect
PARSNIP	Biennial	Insect
PEPPER, SWEET AND HOT	Annual	Insect
PUMPKIN/SQUASH See Table 2	Annual	Insect
SPINACH	Annual	Wind
WATERMELON	Annual	Insect

* Members of one Brassica group will not pollinate members of the other Brassica group.

** Other members of the muskmelon group are not generally grown in the north; e.g., Casaba and Honey Dew.

HARROWSMITH 39

An article on seed saving in 1977 included this table on pollination and recommended that cross-pollinated vegetables be isolated or the seed heads "bagged" in order to retain the purity of the seeds.

Harrowsmith, vol. 2, no. 2 (1977): 39

"A convenient width for each bed in a terrace system is two feet, although we have used widths of four feet successfully. Wider beds, unless they have access from both sides, tend to be more difficult to plant, weed, cultivate and harvest. We did not want to use mortar and confined our terraces to two or three tiers, but more ambitious builders might be inspired to more elaborate creations. Keep in mind, however, that higher terraces are more prone to damage from frost and earth movement in winter."

Stephen S. Tobe and Martha Tobe writing about their experience with city gardens in *Harrowsmith* in 1979.[8]

was a compendium of gardening tips from an 1865 American publication. And the fourth focused on the secrets of shallow planting for earlier germination and better harvests. Gardening articles were often geared to the most basic information, such as "Home Sown Transplants" (issue 18), but readers could also find information on more esoteric gardening possibilities: "Jerusalem Artichokes" (issue 6), "Hops!" (issue 13) and hydroponics in "Adventures in the New Horticulture"(issue 15). In 1978 the magazine also reminded readers of the difficulties the back-to-the-earth movement faced in a special report on "home-steaders who failed."

In 1979 the *Harrowsmith* editors, aware early on that city dwellers made up a significant part of the magazine's market, devoted a whole issue to ideas for city gardeners: "Through judicious use of the land, taking advantage of every square yard, and by employing such techniques as succession planting, terracing, block gardening and the appropriate selection of plant varieties, we've come up with a system by which every city gardener should be able to make the most of his lot."[9] It was a year that city gardens took off. As *The Toronto Star* reported, it was

> the most successful spring ever for garden centres selling seeds and bedding plants, with gardeners in record numbers turning out for their flats of tomatoes, broccoli and sweet peppers. In Kingston, Ontario, the farmers' market closed early on the Saturday of the long Victoria Day weekend, as greenhouse owners were unable to meet the demand and sold out early.[10]

Responding to an obvious dearth of books on gardening in Canada, in 1982 *Harrowsmith* began publishing a series of highly respected titles on various aspects of gardening. Two authors in particular were responsible for books that gardeners continue to rely on—Jennifer Bennett and Patrick Lima. The first gardening title published by Camden House was Jennifer Bennett's *The Harrowsmith Northern Gardener*, which appeared in 1982. In later years she followed this major work with such titles as *The Harrowsmith Landscaping Book*, *The Harrowsmith Annual Garden* and others aimed at specific gardening interests. Patrick Lima's first book was *The Harrowsmith Illustrated Book of Herbs*. Published in 1986, it was a beautifully illustrated book with botanical watercolours by Turid Forsyth. But the book that garden enthusiasts probably refer to most often is Lima's *The Harrowsmith Perennial Garden*, first published in 1987 and still available. The book is based on Larkwhistle, the extensive garden that Lima and his partner have spent years creating on Ontario's Bruce Peninsula. It is both a warm personal account of one garden and a detailed guide to the care and nurturing of a wide range of perennial flowering plants.

Ten years after its amazing beginnings, the first phase of the *Harrowsmith* story came to an end. By then Lawrence had created three other magazines, two of them in the United States, and had moved to Vermont. In 1987 *Harrowsmith* was bought by Telemedia, a large Toronto-based publishing corporation. The magazine continued to be produced from its editorial offices in Camden East for some time, but

SWEET AND FAIR

Garlic chives, BELOW, and chives, RIGHT, are among the most popular herb-garden residents, and rightly so. They are easy to grow from seed or bulb and can be used in any dish that would benefit from a mild onion or garlic flavour.

82

140

A page from *The Harrowsmith Illustrated Book of Herbs*, showing one of Turid Forsyth's elegant illustrations.

The Harrowsmith Illustrated Book of Herbs (Camden East: Camden House, 1986), 82

was later sold to Malcolm Publishing in Montreal. Over the past decade, with the rise of magazines aimed directly at gardeners (discussed in chapter 11), the magazine became less folksy and more broad-ranging in keeping with the times. Its name has changed to *Harrowsmith Country Life*, and the articles continue to cover country life in all its aspects, including the yearly Seed Source Guide and various articles and issues of specific interest to gardeners. ❧

10
Celebrating Our Horticultural Heritage

As more and more new varieties of plants were developed over the decades, two influences turned some gardeners back to the flowers, fruits and vegetables familiar to them from their youth or from earlier documents and seed catalogues. One was a general fear that the diversity of plant life was slowly disappearing; the other was a longing for a simpler, gentler past.

SEEDS OF DIVERSITY

In the United States the Seed Savers Exchange was founded in 1975 as a volunteer organization dedicated to preserving heirloom seeds handed down through generations and in danger of being lost forever. It was inspired by a gift of seeds that Kent and Diane Whealy received from Diane's grandfather. The seeds had been brought from Bavaria four generations earlier; since then, they had been carefully grown and preserved by the family. The Whealys realized that the survival of the varieties of plants from these seeds depended on them. They saw the need for someone to save, not only their seeds, but those from other family collections. Kent began to search them out and thus began the Seed Savers Exchange. By the year 2000, the Seed Savers had 8000 members maintaining thousands of

Joseph Schneider Haus in Kitchener, Ontario, is a "living history" museum, reflecting how a Mennonite farm family lived during the middle of the nineteenth century. The garden illustrated here represents the typical four-square kitchen garden of a traditional Pennsylvania German settler. The four raised beds ensure that the soil warms up quickly in the spring and are edged with annual and perennial herbs to prevent erosion. Flowers, berries, more herbs and vegetables fill the square beds and surrounding borders.

Joseph Schneider Haus

heirloom plants by growing them, saving the seeds, and distributing them to others willing to continue the process.

The same concern for preserving heirloom seeds was being felt in Canada, where some of the members of Seed Savers lived. In 1984 the Canadian Organic Growers (COG) held a conference to discuss the loss of many of the original plant varieties in this country. The COG is a national information network of organic farmers, gardeners and consumers organized to promote the values and methods of organic agriculture and gardening. As a result of this conference, the Heritage Seed Program got underway as a project of COG. It operated this way for a couple of years, but was losing steam until Heather Apple, who had attended the conference, got more seriously involved. The second issue of the magazine she started in 1987 described the goal of the program: "to search out, preserve, share and celebrate our agricultural and horticultural heritage." This would be accomplished by maintaining a living gene bank of endangered plant species, encouraging people to grow heirloom species (from the seed program or from seed companies continuing to offer original, open-pollinated varieties), and making people more aware of "our rich plant heritage."

The appropriately named Heather Apple became the mainstay of the organization. Working out of her home and headquarters in Uxbridge, Ontario, she organized and maintained the gene bank, sent out seeds to the member growers, and wrote most of the magazine, which by 1989 was appearing three times a year. Memberships in the Heritage Seed Program were solicited, and in order to spread the word about the importance of saving seeds of heirloom varieties, members were encouraged to give talks and organize displays in co-operation with historical societies, horticultural groups and garden centres. The program warned of the serious crisis that was arising as a result of the loss of genetic diversity in the foods we eat.

By the end of the 1980s, small individual seed companies throughout North America were being bought up by giant corporations or were going out of business because they were no longer able to compete. Companies such as Monsanto, Dupont and ICI were taking over seed production on a worldwide basis. "When seed companies are taken over," wrote Apple, "their old, regionally adapted, open pollinated varieties are dropped and are replaced by hybrids and patented varieties. Hybrids are more profitable—they are more expensive, people can't save their own seeds, and the parentage of hybrids can be kept secret so that other companies can't reproduce them."[1]

By the end of the 1980s, nearly a thousand varieties were no longer being offered commercially. (All of this was a foreshadowing of more recent concerns about genetic engineering and control of food production by many of the same multinational corporations.) There were other causes for the loss of seed varieties as well. Many families had been growing special varieties of fruits and vegetables for generations. With the modern tendency for people to move frequently, often to apartments or to small city properties where there was little or no room for gardening, these varieties disappeared.

The new seed companies were looking for larger markets and thus catered to commercial growers rather than to home gardeners. Since the requirements for commercial vegetable growers are very different from those of home gardeners, many desirable plant characteristics are being lost. Commercial producers look for crops that ripen all at the same time, respond to chemical fertilizers but resist herbicides and pesticides (all of which the companies sell) and are tough enough to survive mechanical harvesting and long-distance shipping. Home and local producers look for flavour, extended harvests and natural resistance to pests and disease. With this move towards less diversity in plant life, when disease or an infestation of pests destroys crops, the genetic variety that would make it possible to develop new strains might no longer be available.

With the second offering of seeds in 1988, the Heritage Seed Program already had fourteen members

From a few pages in the early issues of the Heritage Seed Program's magazine, by 1998 the yearly seed offering filled its own sixty-five–page issue.

145

offering more than 141 varieties. They were learning through the program how to collect and save seeds and, in particular, how to ensure that the genetic diversity of each variety was maintained. As the Heritage Seed Program magazine began to come out three times a year, other features were added. Members began reviewing heritage or historic gardens in various parts of the country, such as Montgomery's Inn and Joseph Schneider Haus in Ontario, the Grist Mill and Craigflower Farm in British Columbia and the Wallace and Area Museum in Nova Scotia. Seed companies offering heirloom or rare seeds were listed; relevant books were reviewed; and articles devoted to specific fruits, flowers and vegetables—such as Native varieties of corn and Mostoller wild goose beans—were published.

In 1989 the Heritage Seed Program benefited from a five-year grant from the W. Garfield Weston Foundation. Soon other grants came in—from members, other companies and organizations, and government programs, all of which allowed the organization to grow and to extend its influence. The Heritage Seed Program has been represented on the national Expert Committee on Plant Gene Resources, and members work together with Plant Gene Resources of Canada to rejuvenate the gene collection by growing plants to produce seed when stocks are low or seed viability decreases. In the early 1990s the Tsolum

River Fruit Trees Nursery was established in Ganges, British Columbia, with 350 heritage and rare varieties of trees from around the world. It later became a private enterprise, but the Heritage Seed Program continued to encourage and promote private efforts to preserve heritage cultivars and make them available. In 1995 the Heritage Seed Program, which until then had maintained its connection to COG, became independently incorporated, and its name was changed to Seeds of Diversity. Over the years new volunteers

The Annapolis Royal Historic Gardens in Nova Scotia take visitors through four centuries of gardening history, including this replica of an Acadian cottage of 1671. In front of it a "potager," or vegetable garden, can be seen. The garden's unique site, originally Champlain's Port-Royal, overlooks the tidal wetlands and meadows of the Annapolis River as it flows into the Bay of Fundy.

Annapolis Royal Historic Gardens/Photograph by Trish Fry

Upper Canada Village is an authentic re-creation of a typical riverfront community along the St. Lawrence River in the 1860s. Among the typical pioneer gardens of the era is the one at the farmhouse, originally owned by the Loucks. A seed-saving program is maintained to ensure availability of pioneer plant varieties.

Upper Canada Village, c/o The St. Lawrence Parks Commission

have gradually taken on many of the activities that originally fell to Heather Apple, although she remains an active member.

It is fascinating to browse through more than a decade of issues of the Heritage Seed Program, now Seeds of Diversity, magazine and see the growth in professionalism, the increasing sophistication of the plant information, the development of new open-pollinated seed companies such as Gardens North, the promo-tion of seed exchanges and sales ("Seedy Saturdays") across the country, and the ongoing stories of individual members. From its original membership of 120 with 14 offering 141 varieties of seeds, by 2000 it had grown to more than 1500 members offering 1580 distinct varieties of vegetables, flowers, grains and herbs (including 694 varieties of tomatoes!). Of these, about half are not available commercially and would be extinct except for the work of backyard seed savers. "There's security in having a broad gene pool," says Bob Wildfong, who has served as president of Seeds of Diversity, noting the importance of keeping food options open to the many interesting characteristics available in heritage varieties.

WILDFLOWER GARDENS

As more and more gardeners became aware of the importance of maintaining the genetic variety of heirloom plants and seeds, a new interest arose in gardens that benefit the environment. The results were gardens to attract birds and butterflies, gardens based on our own native plants and wildflowers, and gardens that are a part of the natural landscape around them.

The number of generic packages of wildflower seeds that are available now give some idea of how attractive the notion of having our very own meadow can be. Just sprinkle a few packages over the landscape

"While you recommend the attention of the daughters of your subscribers the cultivation of the flowers of the green-house and parterre, be pleased to speak a few words in behalf of the natives of the soil—I mean the lovely Wild Flowers—both as regards their cultivation and their delineation on paper. I am a great admirer of the indigenous flowers of the forest, and it is with a feeling strongly allied to regret, that I see them fading away from the face of the earth ... Man has altered the face of the soil—the mighty giants of the forest are gone, and the lowly shrub, the lovely flower, the ferns and mosses, that flourished beneath their shade, have departed with them."

Catharine Parr Traill in a letter to the
Genesee Farmer in 1852

and gardening chores are over. Unfortunately, it isn't as easy as that! Which is no doubt why few wildflower gardens are in evidence, except those in nature. "Whoever coined the phrase 'Patience is a virtue' could have had wildflower farming in mind,"[2] comments a writer describing how it took one couple four years to establish the right mix of annual and perennial wild plants and grasses to create a self-sustaining native wildflower meadow in Ontario. Most gardeners have neither the space nor the patience to devote to a wildflower meadow, but many opt for something on a smaller scale.

Lorraine Johnson has been one of the most constant and helpful advocates of putting native plants back into the garden. Johnson, the author of a handful of books on the subject, doesn't think that the wildflower garden idea will revolutionize our gardens. "Instead," she says, "I think we'll see a continuation of the slow and steady *evolution* towards native plant gardening. An evolution is much more appropriate anyway. Gradual change, entrenched within the genes, inexorable, unstoppable— that's how it will take hold. As inevitable as water shortages, water restrictions, water metres of pay as you plumb, chemical panics, chemical restrictions, and all the other environmental realities of the 1990s. In other words, we'll slowly see that it makes a lot of sense."[3] Right now she finds a certain irony in the fact that plants that originated in the Far East are more common in our gardens than are our native plants, which tend to be treasured in European gardens.

Johnson recommends staying away from the packaged mixes of wildflowers and, instead, choosing specific native species carefully and collecting seeds in the wild or buying nursery-propagated plants from reputable sources. She lists many sources both for information and for supplying native plants in her book *The Ontario Naturalized Garden*. In it she also describes a visit to an area of original tall-grass prairie maintained by the Walpole Island First Nation on the St. Clair River. This maintenance includes regular burning over of the land. "The variety of species here is astonishing. Botanists have recorded more than eight hundred species of vascular plants on Walpole Island. Of these, approximately one hundred are rare in Ontario and nine have not been found at any other location in Canada."[4]

City and highway planners have begun to see the value in planting wildflowers that seed themselves, do not require cutting and provide touches of roadside colour. Originating in the United States as roadside beautification programs, the idea has been taken up in Canada in recent years. To be successful, these wild gardens must be established using native plant seeds collected from the wild and planted in areas that are as close as possible to their natural habitats:

> The use of wildflowers in parks is a new way of looking at open space potential as productive habitats for the purposes of both man and nature. To be successful it requires changes in the way we look at and design our parks and how we publicize them. The successful implementation of the wildflower

initiatives requires commitment by all parties concerned and a pooling of the talents and skills of botanists, horticulturists and maintenance staff who are willing to learn, share and experiment.[5]

One good way to keep in touch with information on wildflowers and wildflower gardening is through *Wildflower*, a quarterly magazine originated by the Canadian Wildflower Society in 1984 and now published independently.

XERISCAPE GARDENING

One approach to an environmentally friendly garden is xeriscaping—a style of gardening that aims at creating beautiful landscapes that require little or no supplemental watering. Conserving water in the garden depends on a number of elements that good gardeners have always paid attention to: improving the soil to increase its ability to hold water; reducing the size of lawn areas that need extra watering; planting grasses that are drought resistant; grouping plants with similar water requirements; choosing plants that are hardy in the local conditions; and mulching to keep the soil moist longer. As Sara Williams writes in her excellent book *Creating the Prairie Xeriscape*, this is "an environmentally friendly approach to your yard and garden

On the Six Nations Reserve near Brantford, Ontario, Ken and Linda Parker operate Sweet Grass Gardens, the first Native-owned and -operated nursery in North America. Their aim is "to restore, preserve and maintain the pre-European plant species indigenous to North America." The Parkers not only sell seeds and plants, but also arrange tours and give seminars on garden design and growing native and aboriginal plants. Not surprisingly, the difficult-to-find sweet grass (*Hierochloe odorata*) is available here.

Sweet Grass Gardens

which leaves your portion of the world in as good or better shape than when you assumed stewardship."[6] Xeriscaping creates a garden that requires less maintenance, leaving more time to enjoy it.

This same desire to take care of the environment has inspired the cleaning up of rivers, especially where they flow through cities. Planting riverbanks with native plants that once grew there and re-establishing small wetlands where they once existed are both part of this environmentally friendly approach to garden-

ing and landscaping. So, too, with "permaculture," which advocates working with nature rather than fighting it. Instead of using insecticides to kill the aphids that threaten to destroy every rose in the garden, gardeners are encouraged to play host to the insects that feed on aphids, a system that works for many insects. The idea of studying the way nature works and employing the same methods has led to other gardening innovations that we will be hearing more about as time goes by and the need to care for the environment becomes more and more apparent. Some of these involve the use of so-called grey water for irrigation and taking advantage of the ability of plants to clean our air and water.

NATURAL REMEDIES

It is a small leap from here to the increasing interest in growing plants for use as natural remedies. Long recognized as the basis for much folk medicine, herbs are now being studied more seriously for the benefits they might supply: the soothing quality of mint teas; the relief some migraine sufferers experience from feverfew; the relaxing comfort of a bath scented with rosemary or lavender; the healing qualities of aloe vera. Future studies will provide more information to prove or disprove the effectiveness of these ancient remedies. ❧

One recent idea for improving the environment in unhealthy modern office buildings is Genetron's "Breathing Wall Ecosystem." The first large-scale example can be seen in the Canada Life building in downtown Toronto. Described as an indoor rainforest, the wall contains thousands of orchids, bromeliads and airplants. Living within the garden are dozens of fish, shrimp, frogs and mollusks. The result is a natural, self-sustaining system designed to keep the air clean and healthy.

Evergreen Farm, near Kemptville, Ontario, is home to Larry and Anstace Esmonde-White, longstanding hosts of a PBS garden show. Their famous gardens are open to visitors, who can wander past the rock garden to the log cabin, past thriving herb beds and through an arch to the vegetable gardens, and past the bird gazebo before arriving at the Esmonde-White's pride and joy, a full-fledged cedar maze that is a replica of one at the Governor's Palace in Williamsburg, Virginia.

Photograph by Patrick Esmonde-White

11
Gardens, Gardens, Everywhere

What of Canadian gardening in the new millennium? Even though most of us no longer depend on the produce from our own gardens, something continues to draw us to the soil. It can't be just the desire to surround our homes with flowers and shrubs or to experience the fresh taste of vegetables eaten within minutes of their harvest. Statistics Canada calls gardening the fastest growing hobby in Canada (there is the same enthusiasm in the United States, where in a recent survey 40 per cent of Americans described themselves as gardeners). "Gardening competition is so fierce on Victoria Day weekend, you may want to avoid certain downtown streets. It's a jungle in there," warns a recent *Globe and Mail* headline.[1]

In fact, this may not be all good news. In 1999 plants and garden products represented $600 billion in sales. Recently, in both southern British Columbia and southwestern Ontario, people have voiced their concerns about "possibly the hottest trend in farming since the invention of white sliced bread."[2] The tremendous growth in enormous greenhouses is threatening some of the most fertile soil in Canada. All this is in response to Canadians' growing demand for hothouse vegetables and bedding plants.

Plants, catalogues, books, magazines and garden ornaments of one kind or another have become so available, so numerous, that publishers have gone to extremes to get attention. In 1996 *Gardening Life*, a magazine published in Toronto, added a new dimension

One of the country's smallest and most delightful gardens is the Dr. Sun Yat-Sen Classical Chinese Garden in Vancouver's Chinatown. Created on the pattern of a scholar's garden from the Ming Dynasty with materials brought from China, water, rocks, plants and architecture are balanced to create a peaceful, harmonious escape from the bustling world outside.

Dr. Sun Yat-Sen Classical Chinese Garden

Robert Pim Butchart and his wife, Jenny, moved to Vancouver Island in 1904. At Tod Inlet, Mr. Butchart manufactured cement from materials excavated nearby. Jenny Butchart was inspired to create a sunken garden in the quarry that remained behind. The garden continued to grow over the years as the Butcharts added a Japanese garden, an Italian garden and a rose garden. Robert introduced birds of all kinds to the landscape. The Butchart Gardens is among the most famous in the country, with nearly a million visitors each year. Only the tall chimney of the kiln of the original cement factory remains to remind visitors of the gardens' origins.

The Butchart Gardens

to the enjoyment of growing things or, more likely, dreaming of growing things. It was filled with lush, sensuous pictures beautifully reproduced on fine paper and ads for expensive accoutrements for the garden. Books, such as *Shocking Beauty* by Thomas Hobbs of Vancouver, advocate introducing exotic plants and illustrate the electrifying effect of brilliant colours.

The apotheosis of this trend is the magazine *Bloom* from Paris, more properly described as an art publication, which sells for $80 an issue. "People desperately want to hang onto Mother Nature and Human Nature. The more immaterial we become, the more natural we will want to live," writes its editor, Li Edelkoort. Recent articles classify gardening not only as our top pastime, but as a solid investment, citing Japanese maples that sell for up to $50,000 in Toronto! "The going rate for quality landscape projects starts at $10,000 and goes as high as $2 million."[3] (It may be worth remembering that Versailles and its gardens took 36,000 workers twenty-six years to complete.) More and more, the backyard is treated as another room in the house.

Somehow there seems to be no end to the number of times we can read about how to grow better tomatoes (add two crushed Tums to the soil was a recent suggestion), or how to get rid of those pests that eat the heart out of roses just as they open (hand picking still seems to be the most effective). There is always some new trick, some new seed, some old secret rediscovered that makes every article, every chapter, every discussion with the local Master Gardener enticing. As gardening has become more and more an obsession over the past decade, Canadian magazines have been created to fill a need.

READING THE MAGAZINES

Harrowsmith, whose early history is discussed in chapter 9, continues to devote part of each issue to gardens and growing advice, but it has now been joined by magazines completely dedicated to these subjects (along with cooking ideas). *Canadian Gardening* was enthusiastically welcomed by garden addicts when it first appeared early in 1990, just in time to catch the new gardening wave. Now published seven times a year, it has a well-developed line-up with intriguingly named features ("Hello Hosta" or "A Yearning for Yarrow") and articles on landscaping ideas, environmentally friendly insect deterrents, how to create special gardens for special purposes, the latest new seeds and plants, recipes, garden tools, books and house plants. Readers particularly like the "Gardeners Journal" with its regular reports from different regions of the country, which help to solve the problem of

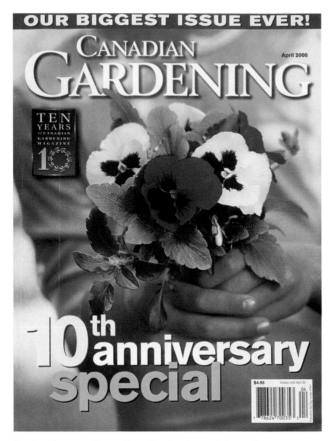

In April 2000, *Canadian Gardening* celebrated ten years of publication with a special issue. "*Canadian Gardening* magazine's first issue in February/March 1990 appeared just as the boom in gardening took off," wrote editor Beckie Fox. "Books, television shows and specialty nurseries were popping up like weeds after a summer rain."[4]

Canadian Gardening, vol.11, no. 2 (April 2000)/Photograph by Burt Klassen

writing for a country with so many climate zones. In 1999 Liz Primeau, the editor for eight years and the person most responsible for the style of the magazine, left to continue her garden writing in other ways, but she continues to contribute her thoughts and ideas on the last page of the magazine. She is also the author of a number of books, including *How to Grow a Butterfly Garden* and *Natural Gardens*.

As it became clear that there was a growing interest to be catered to, two other national magazines (with slightly confusing names) appeared in 1996— *Gardening Life* and *Toronto Life Gardens*. While *Gardening Life* had interesting articles and an attractive look, it seemed to have trouble distinguishing itself in a marketplace where gardening magazines were springing up one after another. (For a time, *Chatelaine* published a yearly special issue called *Chatelaine Gardens!*.) *Toronto Life Gardens*, on the other hand, immediately stood out for its gorgeous photography and design. The question of how it could survive when it was directed so clearly at the Toronto market was answered by the fall when the two magazines merged, creating *Gardening Life*, with their editors, Marjorie Harris and Nancy Jane Hastings, working together.

There are other gardening publications aimed at regional gardeners across the country. Probably the most impressive of these is *Gardens West*, which is published out of Vancouver but covers all of western Canada. *The Gardener for the Prairies* (originally *The Saskatchewan Gardener*) was created in 1995. It is produced by the Extension Division of the University of Saskatchewan, the Saskatchewan Horticultural Association, the Saskatchewan Perennial Society and the Saskatoon Horticultural Society. Inexpensively produced, it concentrates on articles about plants and cultivation for the short growing season and the long, cold winters that gardeners in Manitoba, Saskatchewan and Alberta have to cope with, but its good advice can be usefully followed by anyone.

AND THE WRITERS

With the growth of gardening as a hobby and gardening magazines, it seems only reasonable that the number of writers working in the field would expand, and so they have.

Marjorie Harris holds a dominant position in the world of Canadian garden writing as editor-in-chief of *Gardening Life*. She has also written an astonishing number of books on almost every aspect of gardening, from the lush, large-format *The Canadian Gardener: A Guide to Gardening in Canada* to the pretty, little *The Healing Garden*. Her writing gives the impression that she wants to share every pleasure, every bit of garden lore, with her readers. "My garden is my

The lush quality of the design and photography consistently exhibited by *Gardening Life* is well illustrated in this opening page of an article on growing parrot tulips.

Gardening Life, vol.3, no. 2 (Spring 1999): 65/Photograph by George Whiteside

library, my teacher and guide," she writes, "and it gives me the comfort afforded by little else than a very close and loving family and friends." [5]

Other writers have expanded their careers as garden experts on television. David Tarrant has hosted the CBC television program *The Canadian Gardener* for years, in addition to writing a gardening column and a number of books, and carrying on his work at the University of British Columbia Botanical Garden. Mark Cullen offers garden advice on radio and on the Home and Garden specialty channel on television. He has written a number of gardening books and is president of the family business, Weall and Cullen Nurseries.

Jennifer Bennett and Patrick Lima continue to delight and instruct with new titles. Trevor Cole, for-

A favourite among gardeners for both its writing and its charm, *Tottering in My Garden* has become a classic. Never one for half measures, Midge Keeble attacks her gardening tasks with vigour. "A garden is not the main theme of life," she writes wisely. "It weaves in and out, waits, disappears and reappears, providing a counterpoint to family, home and friends, giving colour and balance to life, challenges unending, and often a dash of the comic." [6]

Tottering in My Garden (Camden East: Camden House, 1989)

mer curator of the Dominion Arboretum and garden at the Central Experimental Farm in Ottawa, has not only produced a number of his own books, but ensures that the Canadian content and information is complete in the encyclopedic books on plants and gardening published by *Reader's Digest*. On the west coast, Des Kennedy is both amusing and accurate in fact and fiction on the subject. Lois Hole, who writes and sells seeds and plants from Alberta, is the author of a long list of valuable titles. Then there are the writers of perhaps only one book on their specialty, such as "the word man," Bill Casselman, and his *Canadian Garden Words* and poet Lorna Crozier and her witty and wonderful *The Sex Lives of Vegetables*. There are a host of other writers, each with his or her own take on gardening or special expertise. Their bylines appear in magazines, newspapers and the books that continue to tempt buyers across the country.

BACK TO THE LAND AGAIN

At the turn of the new century a different kind of move to the country is taking place. In the 1960s and 1970s it was young people searching for a simpler way of life. Now it's comfortable middle-aged city dwellers investing in country property (preferably on water) where they can develop estates for relaxing on weekends and holidays. Here it isn't a matter of trying to live off the land. More often it means an expensive second home with a gardening hobby harking back to earlier times. This movement back to the land has driven up property values within a couple of hundred kilometres of major cities.

Rural life continues, however. A few kilometres farther out property values remain constant, and there young and old still eke out livings that may be close to the poverty line, but that are rich in other values.

WHAT'S HAPPENING TO THE ENVIRONMENT?

Recently a movement to ban the use of so-called cosmetic drugs on lawns, parks and golf courses is gaining steam. Even without an outright ban, slowly but surely, dependence on herbicides, pesticides and fungicides, where they are obviously not essential, is being replaced by less harmful, more organic methods of maintaining the green, grassy swards that people seem to find so desirable.

Since the invention in 1830 of the first lawnmower, which became a popular gardening tool in North America by the end of the nineteenth century, a lush, closely cropped, seamless, weed-free lawn has become a standard feature of the home landscape. It seems likely that over the next decade this kind of lawn will be replaced by more accommodating ground covers.

Wide, grassy steps lead to an unusual stage in the Toronto Music Garden, a beautiful, peaceful spot on the waterfront.

Photograph by Jeremy Martin

ENGINEERING PLANTS GENETICALLY

The most controversial change that farmers and gardeners face at the beginning of the twenty-first century is the introduction of plants that have been genetically modified. Conventional plant breeding uses closely related varieties of a plant to develop new characteristics. In genetic modification (GM), foreign genes are introduced from other vegetable or even animal sources. The claims for agricultural benefits are high, but so far these benefits are unproven. Critics of GM, and there are many, are concerned about the lack of long-term testing, the effect on other plants in nature, our lack of knowledge about how a gene behaves in a new environment, and the control the seed producers are demanding (the new transgenic seeds are available only by licence for one year). These critics are deeply worried about what effect such an unnatural process might have in the long run. Since genetically modified crops have only been grown since 1996, it may be years before any answers are available.

What effect will genetic modification of plants have on the home gardener? Some see this process as a way to make improvements in fruits and vegetables, to create colours that have eluded flower breeders in the past and to create more frost-tolerant species. For now and for some time to come, it seems likely that GM seeds will be aimed at the larger market of commercial growers.

160

GROWING AND SHARING

In 1986 gardeners in Winnipeg decided to donate their extra tomatoes and zucchini to local food banks. This was so obviously a good idea that it was soon picked up in other places. The program, now known as Grow a Row, Plant a Row, was adopted in London, Ontario, where participants planted extra vegetables to pass on to the city's food banks. In 1999 they contributed 22,700 kilograms to the program. By 2000 the Composting Council of Canada was encouraging more gardeners from across the country to take part. One of the nicest things about Grow a Row, Plant a Row is its informal, unstructured approach. Gardeners don't have to make a commitment or register with anyone. They just produce whatever extra vegetables they can and deliver them to the local food bank when they are ready.

On a larger scale, in some communities local farmers are contributing grain grown on unused fields to the World Food Grains Bank. In Belleville, Ontario, local church groups have participated in the program with locally donated land, seed and machinery. Congregation members pitch in to produce the food, which is then distributed throughout the world.

GARDENING IN THE SCHOOLS, AGAIN

New environmental concerns and the desire to encourage children to understand nature and how things grow has inspired a whole new interest in school gardening.

It is unfortunate that just as the new enthusiasm for helping kids create gardens at school is getting underway, cuts to the educational system in many parts of the country are making it harder to sustain. In Toronto, Ossington–Old Orchard Public School

Under the Evergreen school project in British Columbia, students at twenty schools have transformed their schoolyards by planting 1400 native species. These nature areas are used as living classrooms. In this project at the Second Street Community School in Burnaby, students, parents, teachers and others in the community all get involved.

Second Street Community School/Evergreen

students, with the advice of a professional gardener, created a "mini-nature" preserve. On multi-levelled terraces, they planted vegetables, native grasses and even trees, while learning about ecology, composting and such things as native dyes. Budget cuts in 2000 meant that the students lost the expert advice of a professional. However, with the help of the environmentalist Evergreen Foundation, the children will continue to garden.

The Evergreen Foundation is a charity that has been instrumental in encouraging naturalization projects in cities across the country since 1991. In B.C., for instance, one of the projects has involved twenty-one elementary and secondary schools in naturalizing their surroundings with courtyard ponds and plantings; woodland, butterfly and vegetable gardens; bird and wildflower habitats; and even the beginnings of a Douglas fir forest. More than 1000 schools across the country have begun similar projects. Other programs supported by Evergreen (which is funded by government, industry and a host of volunteers) take place in communities as a whole, and even at individual homes. "We are celebrating the start of a new millennium by showing Canadians how we can make a difference," states the organization. "Through the Evergreen Canada Initiative, you can learn what to do to help restore the natural environment in your school, community, or even your own front or back yard—and make our cities greener and healthier."

Evergreen plays a part in many community projects across the country, and community gardening is on the rise in all kinds of ways. In Toronto alone, the number of local community gardens has doubled from twenty to eighty in just four years. The city's Community Garden Network works in different parts of the city to cultivate little-used spaces. Moss Park, a space that had been taken over by drug dealers and prostitutes, became the city's eightieth community garden in the year 2000, adding a note of colour with its flowers and the possibility of fresh produce with its vegetables. A similar project is being undertaken in Toronto's densely populated St. Jamestown. With millennium funding, the new Evergreen Canada Initiative plans to create 2000 public gardens across the country in what is now urban wasteland.

In Saskatoon a garden project that got underway with the help of the city's board of health involves two schools with over 1000 children. They plant container gardens, which they take home to put in the ground when school is over for the summer. The city donated a greenhouse, and the University of Saskatchewan's horticultural department and the Saskatoon Horticultural Society help out. "You need memories of a garden when you were a kid in order to garden as an adult," says the community health nurse who supervises the project.[7]

Another organization aimed at turning Canadian cities into veritable gardens is Communities in Bloom. Since 1995 the program has encouraged villages, towns and cities to improve the landscape with plants, gardens and trees. Competition for the Communities in Bloom awards has encouraged cities and towns from Whitehorse to Charlottetown to work at making nature an integral part of city life, which in turn stimulates civic pride. Cities are judged at the height of the gardening season and awarded points or "blooms" for their efforts.

THERAPEUTIC GARDENING

More and more, gardening is being seen as therapy— no surprise for anyone who has escaped into the garden to forget life's irritations for a time. "The garden provides a wealth of experiences that stimulate thought, exercise the body, nourish the imagination and soothe the soul."[8] Horticultural therapists are beginning to gain status in Canada, where a handful of individuals have received accreditation. The Canadian Horticultural Therapy Association, a volunteer organization incorporated in 1987, now has over 250 members. Horticultural therapy has been

One of the newer gardens in the east, Kingsbrae Garden in St. Andrews-by-the-Sea, New Brunswick, was created in 1998. It incorporated a number of older estates, including their flower beds, cedar hedges and an old-growth forest. In addition to display gardens, a bird and butterfly garden, a therapy garden and demonstration gardens, Kingsbrae Garden is proud of the intricate knot garden seen above.

Kingsbrae Garden

used in working with people suffering from Alzheimer's disease, mental illness, brain injuries and visual impairment, and with children who have cognitive and physical disabilities. The Homewood Health centre in Guelph, Ontario, for instance, treats people with addiction or post-traumatic stress disorders using gardening as therapy. And, for a number of years, the Royal Botanical Gardens has been introducing horticultural programs at hospitals throughout Ontario. Gardens continue to be, as they have been in the past, a comfort to the elderly and the depressed.

STILL MORE GARDENS

It is impossible to do justice to the wonderful and varied gardens that have been created across the country in recent decades. In addition to the botanical gardens described in chapter 7 and the heritage gardens in chapter 10, gardens of special beauty or with special meaning have been created in many centres.

In Lethbridge, Alberta, for instance, the Nikka Yuko Japanese Garden, which opened in 1967, commemorates the evacuation of Japanese Canadians during the Second World War and recognizes their contribution to Canadian culture over the years. Its elegant, authentic character attracts many visitors to the city.

In Toronto the closing of the Don Valley Brick Works offered a rare opportunity for the creation of a

In cities all across the country, small patches of garden illustrating the cultural diversity of the Canadian people flourish in backyards, in front yards, on rooftops and balconies. In Toronto the Seeds of Our City Project is documenting this multicultural activity, exchanging seeds and stories, and recording the food the gardeners grow and how they use it. Vietnamese, Ghanaian and Chinese arc only a few of the immigrant groups sharing their food and their garden expertise and experiences. John Gale, president of Stokes Seeds, credits Canada's immigrants with at least some of the recent increased interest in gardening.

Les Jardins de Métis, or Reford Gardens, is a delightful garden to visit on the south shore of the St. Lawrence River.

Photograph by Malak, Ottawa

park and wetland garden on about sixteen hectares of land within the city. Friends of the Valley, the Garden Club of Toronto, the Canadian Wildlife Society, the Toronto and Region Conservation Authority and many other citizens' groups, foundations and government agencies all helped to turn the area into an attractive garden retreat.

A garden with a much longer history lies on the south shore of the St. Lawrence about 350 kilometres east of Quebec City. Les Jardins de Métis, now designated a National Historic Site and known as Reford

With killing frosts in August and winter temperatures falling to -40° Celsius, gardening in the Yukon is a challenge. John Harmon and his wife, Joyce, live just east of Whitehorse. Here they operate Harmony Farms, growing produce for the local market, and Tropicals North, where even coffee and bananas flourish. These two photographs show the sharp contrast between the stark northern landscape outside the greenhouse and the luscious tomatoes growing within. Harmon's gardening column "The Real Dirt" is available across the country on the Internet.

John Harmon, Harmony Farms

Gardens, was created by Elsie Reford in the 1920s when she was encouraged by her doctor to take up a restful hobby! Over the next thirty years she created one of the finest gardens in Canada. Still managed by the family, it continues to be one of the most enjoyable gardens to visit:

> A rushing brook winds its way through the floral splendour. Gentle slopes, waterfalls and ponds frame picture-perfect arrangements of ever-changing scents and colours. Tall spruce trees shelter the most delicate blooms, displays of exquisite beauty and pathways lead visitors through open glades and leafy arbours, from one memorable visual treat to another. Benches are everywhere, allowing visitors to rest and enjoy the sights and fragrances at their leisure.[9]

Gardens are beginning to improve our cities, not just on the outside but inside buildings and on the streets as well. The Lee Pavilion in Edmonton, a 3700-square-metre tropical garden, adjoins the Citadel Theatre. The sound of the waterfall, the glancing sun from the skylights, the songs of birds and the green of the plants create a haven from the busy city outside.

But the biggest change for gardeners has come, as it has for so many other interests, with the amazing "flowering" of the Internet. So much information is now available without leaving home. Almost all public gardens have their own web sites—some with simple information on where to find them and what their hours are, many with virtual tours that show virtual visitors their favourite plants and most attractive vistas. Sources for seeds are available, and orders can be easily placed. Clubs, societies and personal garden sites abound. Online newsletters describing what's happening in some part of the country (or some part of the world) can easily be found. The Internet is like a walking trail with many side paths. One site leads to another (and sometimes a host of others). What a change from those early pioneer days when gardening discussions could only take place with one or two neighbours or by slow mail!

The world of gardening is at our fingertips, and no doubt amazing changes await gardeners as a new century gets underway. ❧

Notes

CHAPTER 1

1 Nancy J. Turner, *Food Plants of Coastal First Peoples* (Vancouver: University of British Columbia Press, 1995), 43.

2 Olive Patricia Dickason, *Canada's First Nations: A History of Founding Peoples from Earliest Times* (Toronto: McClelland & Stewart, 1992), 37.

3 Henry Youle Hind, *Narrative of the Canadian Red River Exploring Expedition of 1857, and of the Assiniboine and Saskatchewan Exploring Expedition of 1858.* Reprinted from the 1860 edition (Edmonton: Hurtig, 1971), 319.

4 D. Wayne Moodie, "Ojibwa Production of Wild Rice," in *Aboriginal Resource Use in Canada: Historical and Legal Aspects* (Winnipeg: University of Manitoba Press, 1991), 73.

5 *The Shaping of Ontario from Exploration to Confederation* (Belleville: Mika, 1985), 12.

6 Dickason, *Canada's First Nations*, 70.

7 Dickason, *Canada's First Nations*, 26.

8 Dickason, *Canada's First Nations*, 132.

9 Bruce Trigger, *The Huron Farmers of the North* (Toronto: Holt, Rinehart and Winston, 1969), 1.

10 Catherine Flynn and E. Leigh Syms, "Manitoba's First Farmers," *Manitoba History*, Manitoba Historical Society, no. 31 (Spring 1996): 4.

11 Arthur J. Ray, *I Have Lived Here Since the World Began: An Illustrated History of Canada's Native People* (Toronto: Key Porter, 1996), 253.

12 Ray, *I Have Lived Here Since the World Began*, 255.

13 Ray, *I Have Lived Here Since the World Began*, 267.

CHAPTER 2

1 Keith Thomas, *Man and the Natural World* (London: Lane, 1983), 226.

2 Richard Hakluyt, *The First Colonists: Hakluyt's Voyages to North America* (London: Folio Society, 1986), 29-30.

3 Pehr Kalm, *Peter Kalm's Travels in North America*, English version of 1770; revised from the original Swedish and edited by Adolph B. Benson, with a translation of new material from Kalm's diary notes (New York: Wilson-Erickson, 1937).

4 G.P. Holland, "L'Abbé Léon Provancher, 1820-1892," in *Pioneers of Canadian Science: Symposium Presented to*

the *Royal Society of Canada in 1964* (Toronto: University of Toronto Press, 1966), 53.

5 Catharine Parr Traill, with illustrations by Agnes Fitzgibbon, *Studies of Plant Life in Canada: or, Gleanings from Forest, Lake or Plain* (Ottawa: Woodburn, 1885), 68.

6 Carl Berger, *Science, God, and Nature in Victorian Canada* (Toronto: University of Toronto Press, 1983), 36.

7 David Douglas, *Journal Kept by David Douglas During His Travels in North America, 1823-1827 ...* (London: William Wesley, 1914), 68.

8 Quoted in Suzanne Zeller, *Inventing Canada: Early Victorian Science* (Toronto: University of Toronto Press, 1987), 232-33.

9 *The Canadian Biographical Dictionary and Portrait Gallery of Eminent and Self-made Men, Ontario Volume* (Toronto: American Biographical Publishing, 1880), 83.

CHAPTER 3

1 Samuel de Champlain, *The Works of Samuel de Champlain.* Reprint (Toronto: University of Toronto Press, 1971), Vol. I, 301.

2 Champlain, *The Works of Samuel de Champlain*, Vol. I, 327-28.

3 Champlain, *The Works of Samuel de Champlain*, Vol. II, 60.

4 Ethel M.G. Bennett, "Louis Hébert," in *Dictionary of Canadian Biography*, Vol. I (Toronto: University of Toronto Press, 1966), 368.

5 John Fraser, *Historic Canadian Ground: The LaSalle Homestead of 1666 and Other Old Landmarks of French Canada on the Lower Lachine Road* (Montreal: Witness, 1882), 17.

6 Pehr Kalm, *Peter Kalm's Travels in North America.* Revised and edited by Adolph B. Benson (New York: Wilson-Erickson, 1937), Vol. II, 510.

7 Pehr Kalm, *Peter Kalm's Travels in North America*, Vol. II, 510.

8 Quoted in D.W. Moodie, "Gardening on Hudson Bay: The First Century," *The Beaver*, Summer 1978: 54.

9 Quoted in *The Beaver*, Winter 1970: 26.

10 Richard and Janet Lunn, *The County: The First Hundred Years in Loyalist Prince Edward* (Picton: Picton Gazette, 1967), 61.

11 Frank H. Epp, *Mennonites in Canada, 1786-1920* (Toronto: Macmillan, 1974), 76.

12 Susanna Moodie, *Roughing It in the Bush* (London: Bentley, 1852; reprinted Toronto: New Canadian Library, 1989), 489.

13 Catharine Parr Traill, *The Backwoods of Canada: Being Letters from the Wife of an Emigrant Officer, Illustrative of the Domestic Economy of British America* (London: Knight, 1836; reprinted Toronto: New Canadian Library, 1966), 113.

14 Catharine Parr Traill, *The Backwoods of Canada*, 108.

15 Catharine Parr Traill, *The Backwoods of Canada*, 60.

16 Samuel Strickland, *Twenty-seven Years in Canada West; or, The Experiences of an Early Settler* (London: Bentley, 1853), 204-5.

17 H.A. Innis, *Peter Pond: Fur Trader and Adventurer* (Toronto: Irwin & Gordon, 1930), 122.

18 Quoted in *The Beaver*, Winter 1970: 28.

19 Douglas Hill, *The Scots to Canada*, (London: Gentry, 1972), 34.

20 Margaret A. Ormsby, ed. *A Pioneer Gentlewoman in British Columbia: The Recollections of Susan Allison*

(Vancouver: University of British Columbia Press, 1976), 12-13.

21 Andreas Schroeder, *The Mennonites: A Pictorial History of Their Lives in Canada* (Vancouver: Douglas & McIntyre, 1990), 44.

22 W. Kaye Lamb, ed., *Sixteen Years in the Indian Country: The Journal of Daniel Williams Harmon, 1800-1816* (Toronto: Macmillan, 1957), xx.

23 W.W. Thomson, *Gardening in Saskatchewan* (Regina: Reid, 1917), 1.

CHAPTER 4

1 Jacques Mathieu and Eugen Kedl, *The Plains of Abraham: The Search for the Ideal* (Sillery, Quebec: Septentrion, 1993), 178-79.

2 Luella Bruce Creighton, *The Elegant Canadians* (Toronto: McClelland & Stewart, 1967), 79.

3 Robert McNeil, *Practical Tests on Gardening for Manitoba* (Winnipeg: Wilson, 1884), 31.

4 From the original catalogue, reproduced in full in Eileen Woodhead, *Early Canadian Gardening: An 1827 Nursery Catalogue* (Montreal: McGill-Queen's University Press, 1998), 19-36.

5 Gaétan Deschênes, *Histoire de l'horticulture au Québec* (Saint-Laurent, Quebec: Trécarré, 1996), 49. "Ces nouveaux habitants connaissaient déjà les jardins floraux et appliquaient le savoir-faire de leur pays d'origine. Quant aux habitants francophones aux XVIIIe et XIXe siècles, toutes leurs énergies étaient consacrées à construire des habitations et à nourrir les membres de leur famille." (Author's translation in text.)

6 Deschênes, *Histoire de l'horticulture au Québec*, 59. "Nombreux sont les producteurs québécois qui ont profité de sa générosité, de ses conseils et de ses initiatives. Sa vie a été une école d'énergie, d'honnêteté, de travail et de bons exemples dont de nombreux jeunes qui l'entouraient ont su profiter." (Author's translation in text.)

7 Catharine Parr Traill, *The Canadian Settler's Guide* (Toronto: Maclear, 1855; reprint Toronto: New Canadian Library, 1969), 49-50.

8 D.W. Beadle, *Canadian Fruit, Flower, and Kitchen Gardener* (Toronto: James Campbell, 1872), 190.

9 Dorothy Perkins, *The Canadian Garden Book* (Toronto: Thomas Allen, 1918), 104, 108.

10 Perkins, *The Canadian Garden Book*, 13.

11 Perkins, *The Canadian Garden Book*, 14.

12 H.A. Engelhardt, *The Beauties of Nature Combined with Art* (Montreal: Lovell, 1872), x.

CHAPTER 5

1 Richard Allen, *The Social Passion: Religion and Social Reform in Canada 1914-28* (Toronto: University of Toronto Press, 1971), xvii.

2 Edwinna von Baeyer, *Rhetoric and Roses: A History of Canadian Gardening 1900-1930* (Toronto: Fitzhenry & Whiteside, 1984), 2-3.

3 J.R. Wright, *Urban Parks in Ontario, Part II: The Public Park Movement, 1860-1914* (Toronto: Ontario Government, 1984), 1.

4 Quoted in Selwood, Lehr and Cavett, eds. "'The Most Lovely and Picturesque City in All of Canada': The Origins

of Winnipeg's Public Park System," *Manitoba History*, Spring 1960: 24.

5 "Horticulture in Manitoba History," *Manitoba History*, Spring 1996: 14.

6 Reprinted in Edwinna von Baeyer and Pleasance Crawford, eds., *Garden Voices: Two Centuries of Canadian Garden Writing* (Toronto: Random House, 1995), 50.

7 Neil Sutherland, *Children in English-Canadian Society: Framing the Twentieth-Century Consensus* (Toronto: University of Toronto Press, 1978), 194.

8 Herbert F. Sherwood, *Children of the Land: The Story of the Macdonald Movement in Canada* (New York, 1910), 900.

9 *Children's Gardening* (Toronto: Department of Education, 1912).

10 John W. Chalmers, *Schools of the Foothills Province* (Toronto: University of Toronto Press, 1967), 51.

11 Jan Mather, *Designing Alberta Gardens: The Complete Guide to Beautiful Gardens* (Red Deer, Alberta: Red Deer College Press, 1954), 8.

12 W.W. Thompson, *Gardening in Saskatchewan* (Regina: Reid, 1917), 1.

CHAPTER 6

1 Personal communication with Pleasance Crawford, who credits Stephen Otto (both of Toronto) with research on the subject.

2 *Encyclopedia of Gardening* (London, 1850), 341.

3 Joseph Bouchette, *The British Dominions in North America, or, a Topographical and Statistical Description of the Provinces ...* (London: Colburn and Bentley, 1831), 373.

4 Proceedings Connected with the Formation of the Montreal Horticultural Society, and its Constitution (Montreal: The Society, 1847), 9.

5 Quoted in U.P. Hedrick, *A History of Horticulture in America to 1860* (Portland: Timber, 1988), 264.

6 Henry Youle Hind, *Fifty Years' Progress of British North America: Showing the Development of Its Natural Resources ...* (Toronto: Stebbins, 1863), 51.

7 H. Bronson Cowan, Superintendent of Horticultural Societies, quoted in Philip F. Dodds, *The Story of Ontario Horticultural Societies and Their Contribution ...* (Toronto: Ontario Horticultural Association, 1973), 40.

8 Quoted in Dodds, *The Story of Ontario Horticultural Societies*, 27.

9 *Canadian Horticulturist*, vol.1, no. 2 (1878): 31.

10 *Canadian Horticulturist*, vol. 23, no. 3 (1900): 127.

11 Jan Mather, *Designing Alberta Gardens: The Complete Guide to Beautiful Gardens* (Red Deer, Alberta: Red Deer College Press, 1994), 9.

12 Dodds, *The Story of Ontario Horticultural Societies*, 44.

13 Dodds, *The Story of Ontario Horticultural Societies*, part II, 25.

14 W.C. Macoun, Preface to M.H. Howitt, *Beautifying the Home Grounds of Canada* (Ottawa: Department of Agriculture, Canadian Horticultural Council, 1930), 4.

15 Quoted in Dodds, *The Story of Ontario Horticultural Societies*, unpaginated appendix.

16 Carol Matthews, "Let's Go Garden Clubbing," *Canadian Gardening*, vol. 10, no. 7 (December 1999/January 2000): 18.

CHAPTER 7

1 "Landscape architects now on cutting edge of botanical garden's planning," *Pappus* (Royal Botanical Gardens), Autumn 1989: 22.

2 "[J]e reviens pénétré de la nécessité, pour une ville comme la nôtre et pour une université comme celle de Montréal, d'avoir un grand jardin botanique scientifiquement organisé, où l'étudiant comme l'amateur puisse goûter cette joie intime et pure qui monte d'un grand jardin où sont réunies, pour la science et pour l'art, les grandes merveilles de Dieu." Quoted in Gaetan Deschênes, *Histoire de l'horticulture au Québec* (Saint-Laurent: Trécarré, 1996), 107. (Author's translation in text.)

3 "Heaven to Earth: The Montreal Botanical Garden, Insectarium, Biodome and Planetarium," *Muse* (Canadian Museums Association), Spring 1995: 52-53.

4 Maria Newberry House, *Plantae Occidentalis: 200 Years of Botanical Art in British Columbia* (Vancouver: University of British Columbia Botanical Garden, 1979), 33.

CHAPTER 8

1 Henry S. Fry, ed., *Development of Horticulture on the Canadian Prairies: An Historical Review* (Edmonton: Alberta Horticultural Association, 1986; originally published in 1956), 102.

2 T.H. Anstey, *One Hundred Harvests: Research Branch Agriculture Canada 1886-1986.* (Ottawa: Supply and Services, 1986), 78.

3 Anstey, *One Hundred Harvests*, 249.

4 Fred McGuiness, "McKenzie Seeds—A Canadian Tradition." A paper prepared for the company's one hundredth anniversary in 1996.

5 Anstey, *One Hundred Harvests*, 253.

6 Edwinna von Baeyer, "The Horticultural Odyssey of Isabella Preston," *Canadian Horticultural History* (Centre for Canadian Historical Horticultural Studies), vol.1, no.3 (1987): 150.

7 Nicholas Fillmore, *Maritime Radical: The Life and Times of Roscoe Fillmore* (Toronto: Between the Lines, 1992), 31.

8 Fillmore, *Maritime Radical*, 155.

9 Fillmore, *Maritime Radical*, 188.

10 Fillmore, *Maritime Radical*, 224.

11 Jennifer Bennett, "Seedy Characters," in *The Harrowsmith Reader* (Camden East, Ontario: Camden House, 1978), 80.

CHAPTER 9

1 Philip Dodds, *The Story of Ontario Horticultural Societies and Their Contribution ...* (Toronto: Ontario Horticultural Association, 1973), 57.

2 *The Canadian Horticulturist: Floral Edition*, January 1918: 10.

3 Both quotes from *Institute News* (Women's Institutes of Manitoba), March 1940: 1.

4 "The Urban Farmers: Toward a Voluntary Peasanthood," *Harrowsmith*, vol. 3, no. 8 (July 1979): 30.

5 Alan Edmonds, "Would You Give up 25,000 a year to Find 'Peace' Doing Chores on an Island Commune?" *Maclean's*, August 1970: 38-39.

6 Kathlyn Poff, "The Good, the Bad and the Swampy," *The Harrowsmith Reader* (Camden East, Ontario: Camden House, 1978), 8-10.

7 Marcia of Morninglory, *Canadian Whole Earth Almanac*, vol. 1, no. 1 (1970): n.p.

8 Stephen S. Tobe and Martha Tobe, "Small is Bounteous: Improving One's Lot in Life," *Harrowsmith*, vol. 3, no. 8 (July 1979): 43.

9 Tobe and Tobe, "Small is Bounteous": 43.

10 Quoted in "The Urban Farmers: Toward a Voluntary Peasanthood," *Harrowsmith*, vol. 3, no. 8 (July 1979): 30.

CHAPTER 10

1 All quotations in the above paragraphs are taken from *Heritage Seed Program*, vol. 1, no. 2 (December 1988): 2.

2 Tom Cruikshank, "Call of the Wild," *Harrowsmith*, vol. 24, no. 15: 36.

3 Lorraine Johnson, *The Ontario Naturalized Garden: The Complete Guide to Using Native Plants* (Vancouver: Whitecap, 1995), xvi.

4 Lorraine Johnson, *The Ontario Naturalized Garden*, 50.

5 Frank Kershaw, "Metro Makeover," *Wildflower* (Canadian Wildflower Society), vol. 11, no.3 (Summer 1995): 19.

6 Sara Williams, *Creating the Prairie Xeriscape: Low-maintenance, Water-efficient Gardening* (Saskatoon: University of Saskatchewan, 1997), 1.

CHAPTER 11

1 *Globe and Mail*, 20 May 2000, R24.

2 *Globe and Mail*, 4 July 2000, A3.

3 *Globe and Mail*, 10 June 2000, R4.

4 *Canadian Gardening*, vol. 11, no. 2 (April 2000): 8.

5 Marjorie Harris, *In the Garden: Thoughts on Changing Seasons* (Toronto: HarperCollins, 1995), n.p.

6 Midge Ellis Keeble, *Tottering in My Garden: A Gardener's Memoir* (Camden East, Ontario: Camden House, 1989), 3.

7 Sara Williams, "Hort Therapy: It's Just a Garden Project!" *The Saskatchewan Gardener*, vol. 1, no. 4 (Fall/Winter 1995): 30.

8 Karen York, "Stake Two Asters and Call Me in the Morning," *Gardening Life*, Fall 1999: 51.

9 John MacDonald, "Quebec's Floral Splendour: Les Jardins de Métis," *Carp News*, May 1998: 31.

Selected Bibliography

GENERAL TITLES

Bisgrove, Richard. *The National Trust Book of the English Garden*. London: Penguin, 1992.

Canadian Gardening. Markham, Ontario: Avid Media.

Canadian Horticultural History: An Interdisciplinary Journal. Vols. 1-3. Hamilton: Centre for Canadian Historical Horticultural Studies, Royal Botanical Gardens, 1985-1995.

Canadian Horticulturist. St. Catharines: Fruit Growers' Association of Ontario, 1874-1914; Floral Edition Peterboro [sic], 1915–1938.

Deschênes, Gaétan. *Histoire de l'horticulture au Québec*. Saint-Laurent, Quebec: Trécarré, 1996.

Fry, Harold S, ed. *Development of Horticulture on the Canadian Prairies: An Historical Review*. Saskatoon: Western Canadian Society for Horticulture, 1956; reprinted Alberta Horticultural Association, 1986.

Gardening Life. Toronto: Gardening Life Publishing.

Harrowsmith. Camden East, Ontario, 1976–87.

Heritage Seed Program/Seeds of Diversity magazine. Toronto.

"Horticulture in Manitoba History." *Manitoba History*. Manitoba Historical Society. No. 31 (Spring 1996).

Johnson, Hugh. *The Principles of Gardening*. New York: Simon & Schuster, 1979.

Leighton, Ann. *American Gardens of the Eighteenth Century: "For Use or for Delight."* Amherst: University of Massachusetts, 1987.

— *American Gardens of the Nineteenth Century: "For Comfort and Affluence."* Amherst: University of Massachusetts, 1987.

Pappus. Hamilton: Royal Botanical Gardens.

Quatre-Temps. Montreal: Les Amis du jardin botanique de Montréal.

The Saskatchewan Gardener. Saskatoon: The Saskatchewan Gardener.

von Baeyer, Edwinna. *Rhetoric and Roses: A History of Canadian Gardening 1900-1930*. Toronto: Fitzhenry & Whiteside, 1984.

— *A Selected Bibliography for Garden History in Canada*. Ottawa: Environment Canada, 1987.

— and Pleasance Crawford, eds. *Garden Voices: Two Centuries of Canadian Garden Writing*. Toronto: Random, 1995.

Whiteman, Bruce. "Early Canadian Gardeniana." *The Whig-Standard Magazine*. Vol.10, no. 27 (22 April 1989).

Van Zuylen, Gabrielle. *Tous les jardins du monde*. Paris: Gallimard, 1994.

CHAPTER 1

Abel, Kerry and Jean Friesen. *Aboriginal Resource Use in Canada: Historic and Legal Aspects*. Winnipeg: University of Manitoba, 1991.

Cameron, Christibe and Jean Trudel. *The Drawings of James Cockburn: A Visit Through Quebec's Past*. Toronto: Gage, 1976.

Dickason, Olive Patricia. *Canada's First Nations: A History of Founding Peoples from Earliest Times*. Toronto: McClelland & Stewart, 1992.

Du Creux, Father François. *Historiae Canadensis ...* Paris, 1664.

Flynn, Catherine and E. Leigh Syms, "Manitoba's First Farmers." *Manitoba History*. Manitoba Historical Society. No. 31 (Spring 1996), 4.

Heidenreich, Conrad. *Huronia: A History and Geography of the Huron Indians, 1600-1650*. Toronto: McClelland & Stewart, 1971.

Hind, Henry Youle. *Narrative of the Canadian Red River Exploring Expedition of 1857, and of the Assiniboine and Saskatchewan Exploring Expedition of 1858*. Reprinted from the 1860 edition. Edmonton: Hurtig, 1971.

Ray, Arthur J. *I Have Lived Here Since the World Began: An Illustrated History of Canada's Native People*. Toronto: Key Porter, 1996.

Rogers, Edward S. and Donald B. Smith. *Aboriginal Ontario: Historical Perspectives on the First Nations*. Toronto: Dundurn, 1994.

The Shaping of Ontario from Exploration to Confederation. Belleville, Ontario: Mika, 1985.

Trigger, Bruce G. *The Huron Farmers of the North*. Toronto: Holt, Rinehart and Winston, 1969.

— *Natives and Newcomers: Canada's "Heroic Age" Reconsidered*. Montreal: McGill-Queen's University Press, 1985.

Turner, Nancy J. *Food Plants of Coastal First Peoples*. Vancouver: University of British Columbia Press, 1995.

Waugh, F.W. *Iroquois Foods and Food Preparation*. Ottawa: Geological Survey, 1916, 1973.

CHAPTER 2

Berger, Carl. *Science, God, and Nature in Victorian Canada*. Toronto: University of Toronto Press, 1983.

The Canadian Biographical Dictionary and Portrait Gallery of Eminent and Self-made Men, Ontario Volume. Toronto: American Biographical Publishing, 1880.

de Charlevois, Pierre-François. *Histoire et description générale de la Nouvelle France: avec le journal historique d'un voyage fait par ordre du Roi ... Tome II* . Paris: Rolin fils, 1744.

Cornut, Jacques-Philippe. *Canadensium Plantarum Historia*. Paris: Venundantur apud Simonem Le Moyne, 1635.

Couture, Pierre. *Marie-Victorin: le botaniste patriote*. Montreal: XYZ, 1996.

Douglas, David. *Journal Kept by David Douglas During His Travels in North America, 1823-1827 ...* London: William Wesley, 1914.

Downie, Mary Alice and Mary Hamilton. *"And some brought flowers."* Illustrations by E.J. Revell. Toronto: University of Toronto Press, 1980.

Hakluyt, Richard. *The First Colonists: Hakluyt's Voyages to North America*. London: Folio Society, 1986.

House, Maria Newberry. *Plantae Occidentalis: 200 Years of Botanical Art in British Columbia*. Vancouver: Botanical Garden, University of British Columbia, 1979.

Houston, Stuart C., ed. *Arctic Artist: The Journal and Paintings of George Back, Midshipman with Franklin, 1819-1822*. Montreal: McGill-Queen's University Press, 1994.

Kalm, Pehr. *Peter Kalm's Travels in North America*. English version of 1770 revised from the original Swedish and edited by Adolph B. Benson. New York: Wilson-Erickson, 1937.

Lafitau, Joseph-François. *Mémoire présenté a Son Altesse Royale Mgr. le duc D'Orléans, régent de France, concernant la précieuse plante du gin-seng ...* Paris: Mongé, 1718.

Macoun, John. *Autobiography of John Macoun, Canadian Explorer and Naturalist, Assistant Director and Naturalist to the Geological Survey of Canada, 1831-1920*. Ottawa: Ottawa Field Naturalists Club, 1922.

Marie-Victorin, Frère. *Flore laurentienne*. Montreal: La Salle, 1935.

Montgomery, F.H. *Plants from Sea to Sea*. Toronto: Ryerson Press, 1966.

Morris, Maria. *Wildflowers of Nova Scotia*. Botanical information by Titus Smith. Halifax: Belcher, 1840.

Penhallow, D.P. *A Review of Canadian Botany, 1800 to 1895*. Papers from the Department of Botany, McGill University, no. 7. Montreal: Transactions of the Royal Society of Canada, 1898.

Pioneers of Canadian Science, Symposium Presented to the Royal Society of Canada in 1964. Toronto: University of Toronto Press, 1966.

Provancher, Abbé Léon. *Traité élémentaire de botanique*. Quebec: St. Michel et Darveau, 1858.

Saunders, Gill. *Picturing Plants: An Analytical History of Botanical Illustration*. Los Angeles: University of California Press, 1995.

Taylor, Roy L. and R.A. Ludwig, eds. *The Evolution of Canada's Flora*. Toronto: University of Toronto Press, 1966.

Thomas, Keith. *Man and the Natural World*. London: Lane, 1983.

Traill, Catharine Parr. *Canadian Wild Flowers*. Illustrations by Agnes Fitzgibbon. Montreal: Lovell, 1868.

— *Studies of Plant Life in Canada: or, Gleanings from Forest, Lake or Plain*. Illustrations by Agnes Fitzgibbon. Ottawa: Woodburn, 1885.

Trew, Christoph Jakob. *The Herbal of the Count Palatine: An Eighteenth Century Herbal*. Illustrations by Elizabeth Blackwell and Georg Dionysius Ehret. London: Harrap, 1985.

Waiser, W.A. *The Field Naturalist: John Macoun, the Geological Survey, and Natural Science*. Toronto: University of Toronto Press, 1989.

Zeller, Suzanne. *Inventing Canada: Early Victorian Science*. Toronto: University of Toronto Press, 1987.

CHAPTER 3

Bartlett, W.H. *Canadian Scenery*. Illustrated. Vol. II. London: Virtue, undated; facsimile edition Toronto: Peter Martin, 1967.

The Beaver. Winter 1970.

Bocking, D.H., ed. *Saskatchewan: A Pictorial History*. Saskatoon: Western Producer, 1979.

Careless, J.M.S. *The Pioneers: The Picture Story of Canadian Settlement*. Toronto: McClelland & Stewart, 1968.

de Champlain, Samuel. *Voyages du Sieur de Champlain ...* Paris: Berjon, 1613.

— *The Works of Samuel de Champlain*. Reprint. Vols. I, II. Toronto: University of Toronto Press, 1971.

Dictionary of Canadian Biography. Vol. I. Toronto: University of Toronto Press, 1966.

Eccles, W.J. *The Canadian Frontier: 1534-1760*. Toronto: Holt, Rinehart and Winston, 1969.

Epp, Frank H. *Mennonites in Canada, 1786-1920*. Toronto: Macmillan, 1974.

Fraser, John. *Historic Canadian Ground: The LaSalle Homestead of 1666 and Other Old Landmarks of French Canada on the Lower Lachine Road*. Montreal: Witness, 1882.

Hill, Douglas. *The Scots to Canada*. London: Gentry, 1972.

Hind, Henry Youle. *Narrative of the Canadian Red River Exploring Expedition of 1857, and of the Assiniboine and Saskatchewan Exploring Expedition of 1858*. London: Longman, 1860; reprinted Edmonton: Hurtig, 1971.

Innis, H.A. *Peter Pond: Fur Trader and Adventurer*. Toronto: Irwin & Gordon, 1930.

Lamb, W. Kaye, ed. *Sixteen Years in the Indian Country: The Journal of Daniel Williams Harmon, 1800-1816*. Toronto: Macmillan, 1957.

Lunn, Richard and Janet Lunn. *The County: The First Hundred Years in Loyalist Prince Edward*. Picton, Ontario: Picton Gazette, 1967.

Major, Marjorie. *From the Ground: The Story of Planting in Nova Scotia*. Halifax: Petheric, 1981.

Moodie, D.W. "Gardening on Hudson Bay: The First Century." *The Beaver*. Summer 1978: 54.

Moodie, Susanna. *Roughing It in the Bush*. London: Bentley, 1852; reprinted Toronto: New Canadian Library, 1989.

Moore, Christopher. *The Loyalists*. Toronto: Macmillan, 1984.

Ouellet, Fernand. *Lower Canada, 1791-1840: Social Change and Nationalism*. Toronto: McClelland & Stewart, 1980.

Ormsby Margaret, ed. *A Pioneer Gentlewoman in British Columbia: The Recollections of Susan Allison*. Vancouver: University of British Columbia Press, 1976.

Schroeder, Andreas. *The Mennonites: A Pictorial History of Their Lives in Canada*. Vancouver: Douglas & McIntyre, 1990.

Strickland, Samuel. *Twenty-seven Years in Canada West; or, The Experiences of an Early Settler*. London: Bentley, 1853.

Thomson, W.W. *Gardening in Saskatchewan*. Regina: Reid, 1917.

Traill, Catharine Parr. *The Backwoods of Canada: Being Letters from the Wife of an Emigrant Officer, Illustrative of the Domestic Economy of British America*. London: Knight, 1836; reprinted Toronto: New Canadian Library, 1966.

Trueman, Stuart. *An Intimate History of New Brunswick*. Toronto: McClelland & Stewart, 1970.

Wilson, Bruce. *As She Began: An Illustrated Introduction to Loyalist Ontario*. Toronto: Dundurn, 1981.

CHAPTER 4

Beadle, D.W. *Canadian Fruit, Flower, and Kitchen Gardener*. Toronto: James Campbell, 1872.

Crawford, Pleasance. "Henry A. Engelhardt (1830-1897): Landscape Designer." Paper for a symposium of the German-Canadian Historical Association at the University of Guelph, 5 June 1984.

Creighton, Luella Bruce. *The Elegant Canadians*. Toronto: McClelland & Stewart, 1967.

Dougall, James. *The Canadian Fruit-culturist; or, Letters to an Intending Fruit-grower*. Montreal: Dougall, 1867.

Drummond, William Henry. *Montreal in Halftone: A Souvenir*. Montreal: Clarke, 1900.

Engelhardt, H.A. *The Beauties of Nature Combined with Art*. Montreal: Lovell, 1872.

Illustrated Historical Atlas of Hastings and Prince Edward Counties. Toronto: Meacham, 1878; reprinted Belleville, Ontario: Mika, 1972.

Illustrated Historical Atlas of Prince Edward Island. Toronto: Meacham, 1880; reprinted Belleville, Ontario: Mika, 1972.

Lounsberry, Alice. *A Guide to the Trees*. Toronto: Briggs, 1900.

McNeil, Robert. *Practical Tests on Gardening in Manitoba*. Winnipeg: Wilson, 1884.

Martin, Paul-Louis. *Promenades dans les jardins anciens du Québec*. Photographs by Janouk Murdock. Montreal: Boréal, 1996.

Mathieu, Jacques and Eugene Kedl. *The Plains of Abraham: The Search for the Ideal*. Sillery, Quebec: Septentrion, 1993.

Minhinnick, Jeanne. *At Home in Upper Canada*. Toronto: Stoddart, 1970.

Perkins, Dorothy. *The Canadian Garden Book*. Toronto: Thomas Allen, 1918.

Scott, Owen R. "The Lily, the Locust, and the Lilac." An unpublished address given at A Symposium on Garden History in Southern Ontario. Toronto: Archives of Ontario. Pamphlet no.99 (1984).

Woodhead, Eileen. *Early Canadian Gardening: An 1827 Nursery Catalogue*. Montreal: McGill-Queen's University Press, 1998.

CHAPTER 5

Allen, Richard. *The Social Passion: Religion and Social Reform in Canada, 1914-28*. Toronto: University of Toronto Press, 1971.

Callwood, June. *The Naughty Nineties 1890/1900*. Toronto: Natural Science, 1977.

Canadian Pacific Railway Bulletin. Montreal, 1916-1946.

Chalmers, John W. *Schools of the Foothills Province*. Toronto: University of Toronto Press, 1967.

Children's Gardening. Toronto: Department of Education, 1912.

Cook, Ramsay. *The Regenerators: Social Criticism in Late Victorian English Canada*. Toronto: University of Toronto Press, 1985.

"Horticulture in Manitoba History." *Manitoba History*. Spring 1996: 14.

Howitt, M.H. *Beautifying the Home Grounds of Canada*. Canadian Horticultural Council. Ottawa: Department of Agriculture, 1930.

Martin, Linda and Kerry Seagrave. *City Parks of Canada*. Oakville, Ontario: Mosaic, 1983.

Mather, Jan. *Designing Alberta Gardens: The Complete Guide to Beautiful Gardens*. Red Deer, Alberta: Red Deer College Press, 1954.

Rybczynski, Witold. *A Clearing in the Distance: Frederick*

Law Olmsted and North America in the Nineteenth Century. Toronto: HarperFlamingo, 1999.

Selwood, Lehr and Cavett, eds. "'The Most Lovely and Picturesque City in All of Canada': The Origins of Winnipeg's Public Park System." *Manitoba History*. Spring 1960: 24.

Sutherland, Neil. *Children in English-Canadian Society: Framing the Twentieth-Century Consensus*. Toronto: University of Toronto Press, 1978.

Sherwood, Herbert F. *Children of the Land: The Story of the Macdonald Movement in Canada*. New York, 1910.

Wright, J.R. *Urban Parks in Ontario*. Part II: *The Public Park Movement, 1860-1914*. Toronto: Government of Ontario, 1984.

CHAPTER 6

Bouchette, Joseph. *The British Dominions in North America, or, a Topographical and Statistical Description of the Provinces ...* London: Colburn and Bentley, 1831.

Stevens, L.R. *The Canadian Horticultural Council: Fifty Years of Integrity, Leadership and Liaison*. Ottawa, 1972.

Dodds, Philip F. *The Story of Ontario Horticultural Societies and Their Contribution to Making the Province a More Beautiful and Better Place to Live, 1854-1973*. Toronto: Ontario Horticultural Association, 1973.

Encyclopedia of Gardening. London, 1850.

Hambleton, Margaret. *Nova Scotia Association of Garden Clubs: The First Twenty Years, 1954-1973*. Truro, Nova Scotia: The Association, 1973.

Hedrick, U.P. *A History of Horticulture in America to 1860*. London: Oxford, 1950; reprinted Portland, Oregon: Timber, 1988.

Hind, Henry Youle. *Fifty Years' Progress of British North America: Showing the Development of Its Natural Resources ...* Toronto: Stebbins, 1863.

Proceedings Connected with the Formation of the Montreal Horticultural Society, and its Constitution. Montreal: The Society, 1847.

CHAPTER 7

Anstey, T.H. *One Hundred Harvests: Research Branch, Agriculture Canada, 1886-1986*. Ottawa: Supply and Services, 1986.

Bouchard, André. *Le Jardin botanique de Montréal: esquisse d'une histoire*. Saint-Laurent, Quebec: Fides, 1998.

Bridge, Josephine. *The University of British Columbia Botanical Garden*. Vancouver: The Botanical Garden, 1993.

Fifty Years of Progress on Dominion Experimental Farms: 1886-1936. Ottawa: Department of Agriculture, 1936.

Fyles, Faith. *Principal Poisonous Plants of Canada*. Ottawa: Taché, 1920.

"Heaven to Earth: The Montreal Botanical Garden, Insectarium, Biodome and Planetarium." *Muse*. Canadian Museums Association. Spring 1995: 52-53.

"Landscape architects now on cutting edge of botanical garden's planning." *Pappus*. Royal Botanical Gardens. Autumn 1989: 22.

Smith, Helen. *Ottawa's Farm: A History of the Central Experimental Farm*. Photographs by Mary Bramley. Burnstown, Ontario: General Store, 1996.

Stubbs, Betty. *From Golf Course to Garden: A History of VanDusen Botanical Display Gardens*. Vancouver: VanDusen Botanical Garden, 1985.

Track, Norman S. *Canada's Royal Garden: Portraits and Reflections.* Illustrations by Gerard Brender à Brandis. Toronto: Viking, 1994.

CHAPTER 8

Ainley, Marianne Gosztonyi, ed. *Despite the Odds: Essays on Canadian Women and Science.* Montreal: Véhicule, 1990.

Canadian Horticultural History. Centre for Canadian Historical Horticultural Studies. Vols. 1-3 (1985-95).

Canadian Nurseryman Centennial Yearbook 1967. Ottawa.

Fillmore, Nicholas. *Maritime Radical: The Life and Times of Roscoe Fillmore.* Toronto: Between the Lines, 1992.

Fillmore, Roscoe. *Roses for Canadian Gardens.* Toronto: Ryerson Press, 1959.

— *Green Thumbs.* Toronto: Ryerson Press, 1953.

— *The Perennial Border and Rock Garden.* Toronto: Ryerson Press, 1961.

Horticultural Horizons: Plant Breeding and Introduction at Dropmore, Manitoba. Manitoba: Department of Agriculture and Conservation, 1967.

Preston, Isabella. *Herbaceous Perennials; With Lists of Varieties for Special Purposes and Districts.* Ottawa: Department of Agriculture, 1929.

— *Hardy Roses: Their Culture in Canada.* Ottawa: Department of Agriculture, 1935.

— *Lilies for Every Garden.* New York: Orange Judd, 1947.

Ronald, W.G.,ed. *The Development of Manitoba's Nursery and Landscape Industry, 1957-1982.* Winnipeg: Manitoba Nursery and Landscape Association, 1983.

Track, Norman S. *Canada's Royal Garden: Portraits and Reflections.* Toronto: Viking, 1994.

von Baeyer, Edwinna. "The Horticultural Odyssey of Isabella Preston." *Canadian Horticultural History.* Centre for Canadian Historical Horticultural Studies. Vol.1, no.3 (1987): 150.

Yeager, William. *A Century of Gardening: Simcoe and District Horticultural Society, 1896-1996.* Simcoe, Ontario: Simcoe and District Horticultural Society, 1996.

Zeller, Suzanne. *Inventing Canada: Early Victorian Science.* Toronto: University of Toronto Press, 1987.

CHAPTER 9

Bennett, Jennifer. *The Harrowsmith Northern Gardener.* Camden East, Ontario: Camden House, 1982.

— *The Harrowsmith Tomato Handbook.* Camden East, Ontario: Camden House, 1985.

— and Turid Forsyth. *The Harrowsmith Annual Garden.* Camden East, Ontario: Camden House, 1990.

Canadian Whole Earth Almanac. Toronto: Canadian Whole Earth Research Foundation. Vols.1-3 (1970-72).

Edmonds, Alan. "Would You Give up 25,000 a Year to Find 'Peace' Doing Chores on an Island Commune?" *Maclean's.* August 1970: 38-39.

The Harrowsmith Reader. Camden East, Ontario: Camden House, 1978.

Harvey, David D. *Americans in Canada: Migration and Settlement Since 1840.* Queenston, Ontario: Mellen, 1991.

Institute News. Women's Institutes of Manitoba. March 1940.

Lima, Patrick. *The Harrowsmith Illustrated Book of Herbs.* Illustrations by Turid Forsyth. Camden East, Ontario: Camden House, 1986.

— *Perennial Garden: Flowers for Three Seasons.* Camden East, Ontario: Camden House, 1987.

Sutherland, Fraser. *The Monthly Epic: A History of Canadian Magazines.* Toronto: Fitzhenry & Whiteside, 1989.

Tobe, Stephen S. and Martha Tobe. "Small is Bounteous: Improving One's Lot in Life." *Harrowsmith.* Vol. 3, no. 8 (July 1979): 43.

"The Urban Farmers: Toward a Voluntary Peasanthood." *Harrowsmith.* Vol. 3, no. 8 (July 1979): 30.

Wilson, Lois. *Chatelaine's Gardening Book: The Complete All-Canada Guide to Garden Success.* Toronto: Doubleday, 1970.

CHAPTER 10

Ballstadt, Carl, Elizabeth Hopkins, and Michael A. Peterman, eds., *I Bless You in My Heart: Selected Correspondence of Catharine Parr Traill.* Toronto: University of Toronto Press, 1996.

Bennett, Jennifer. *Dry-Land Gardening: A Xeriscaping Guide for Dry-Summer, Cold-Winter Climates.* Willowdale, Ontario: Firefly, 1998.

Canadian Gardening's Natural Gardens. Toronto: Madison, 1996.

Cruikshank, Tom. "Call of the Wild." *Harrowsmith.* Vol. 24, no. 15: 36.

Heritage Seed Program. Vol.1, no. 2 (December 1988): 2.

Johnson, Lorraine. *The Ontario Naturalized Garden: The Complete Guide to Using Native Plants.* Vancouver: Whitecap, 1995.

Kershaw, Frank. "Metro Makeover." *Wildflower.* Canadian Wildflower Society. Vol. 11, no.3 (Summer 1995): 19.

Williams, Sara. *Creating the Prairie Xeriscape: Low-maintenance, Water-efficient Gardening.* Saskatoon: University of Saskatchewan, 1997.

CHAPTER 11

Melhorn-Boe, Lisa and Lorna Crozier. *The Sex Lives of Vegetables: A Seed Catalogue.* North Bay, Ontario: Transformer, 1990.

Canadian Gardening. Vol.11, no. 2 (April 2000): 8.

Casselman, Bill. *Canadian Garden Words.* Toronto: Little Brown, 1997.

Chambers, Douglas. *Stony Ground: The Making of a Canadian Garden.* Toronto: Knopf, 1996.

Crozier, Lorna. *The Garden Going on Without Us.* Toronto: McClelland & Stewart, 1985.

Fawcett, Brian. *The Compact Garden: Discovering the Pleasures of Planting in a Small Place.* Camden East, Ontario: Camden House, 1992.

Globe and Mail, 20 May 2000, R24.

Globe and Mail, 10 June 2000, R4.

Globe and Mail, 4 July 2000, A3.

Harris, Marjorie. *Favorite Perennials.* Photographs by Paddy Wales. Toronto: HarperCollins, 1994.

— *The Canadian Gardener: A Guide to Gardening in Canada.* Photographs by Tim Saunders. Toronto: Random, 1990.

— *The Healing Garden: Nature's Restorative Powers.* Toronto: HarperCollins, 1996.

— *In the Garden: Thoughts on Changing Seasons.* Toronto: HarperCollins, 1995.

Keeble, Midge Ellis. *Tottering in My Garden: A Gardener's Memoir.* Camden East, Ontario: Camden House, 1989.

MacDonald, John. "Quebec's Floral Splendour: Les Jardins de Métis." *Carp News*, May 1998: 31.

Powning, Beth. *Home: Chronicle of a North Country Life.* New York: Stewart, Tabori and Chang, 1996.

Prieur, Benoit. *Guide des beaux jardins du Québec.* La Prairie, Quebec: Broquet, 1992.

Tarrant, David. *David Tarrant's Canadian Gardens.* Vancouver: Whitecap, 1994.

York, Karen. "Stake Two Asters and Call Me in the Morning." *Gardening Life.* Fall 1999: 51.

von Baeyer, Edwinna. *Garden of Dreams: Kingsmere and Mackenzie King.* Toronto: Dundurn, 1990.

Williams, Sara. "Hort Therapy: It's Just a Garden Project!" *The Saskatchewan Gardener.* Vol. 1, no. 4 (Fall/Winter 1995): 30.

Index

This book was printed in Canada by St. Joseph M.O.M. Printing
Typesetting: Donna Bates
Typeface: Trump Mediäval and Hiroshige
Paper: Horizon Silk 80 lb.
Book design: Miriam Bloom

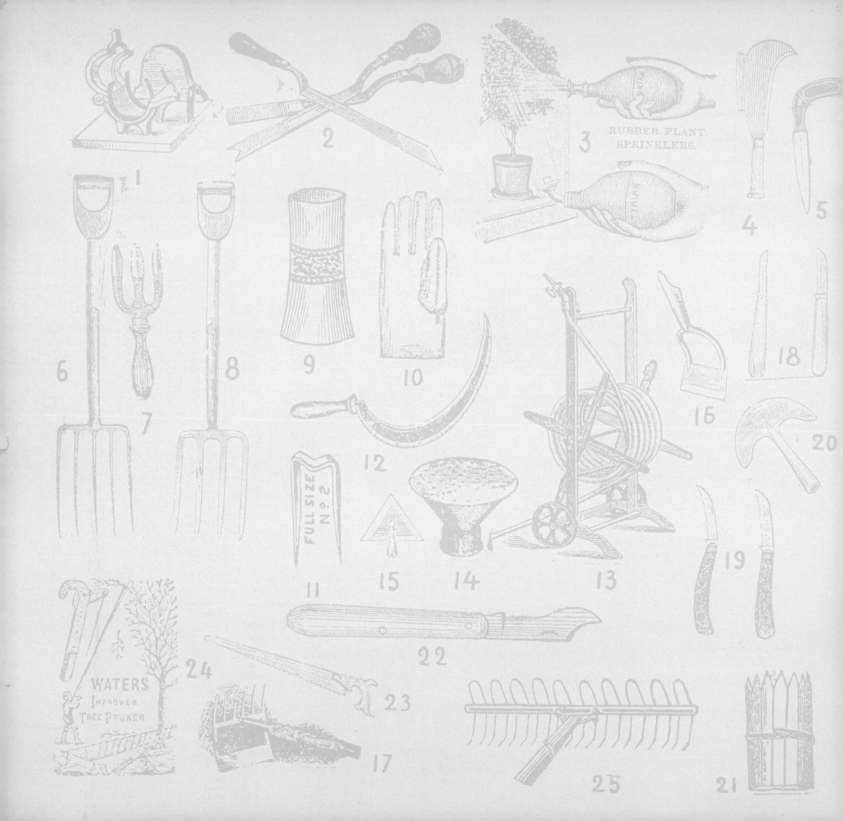

1

2

3 RUBBER PLANT SPRINKLERS.

4

5

6

7

8

9

10

11

12

FULL SIZE No. 2

15

14

13

16

18

20

19

WATERS IMPROVED TREE PRUNER

24

23

17

22

25

21